ON ANGER

Editors-in-Chief Deborah Chasman & Joshua Cohen

Executive Editor Chloe Fox

Managing Editor and Arts Editor Adam McGee

Senior Editor Matt Lord

Engagement Editor Rosie Gillies

Contributing Editors Junot Díaz, Adom Getachew, Walter Johnson, Robin D.G. Kelley, Lenore Palladino

Contributing Arts Editors Ed Pavlić & Evie Shockley

Editorial Assistant Thayer Anderson

Marketing and Development Manager Dan Manchon

Finance Manager Anthony DeMusis III

Distributor The MIT Press, Cambridge, Massachusetts, and London, England

Printer Sheridan PA

Board of Advisors Derek Schrier (chairman), Archon Fung, Deborah Fung, Alexandra Robert Gordon, Richard M. Locke, Jeff Mayersohn, Jennifer Moses, Scott Nielsen, Robert Pollin, Rob Reich, Hiram Samel, Kim Malone Scott

Interior Graphic Design Zak Jensen & Alex Camlin

Cover Design Alex Camlin

On Anger is *Boston Review* Forum 13 (45.1)

To become a member, visit:
bostonreview.net/membership/

For questions about donations and major gifts,
contact: Dan Manchon, dan@bostonreview.net

For questions about memberships, call 877-406-2443
or email Customer_Service@bostonreview.info.

Boston Review
PO Box 425786, Cambridge, MA 02142
617-324-1360

ISSN: 0734-2306 / ISBN: 978-1-946511-54-6

CONTENTS

EDITORS' NOTE
Deborah Chasman & Joshua Cohen

"FEEL GOOD. Feel better. Move forward. Let it go," Claudia Rankine writes in her poem *Citizen*, in the internal monologue of a black woman trying to move past anger over racial wrongs.

Rankine depicts a familiar sensibility about anger: yes, we sometimes have good reason for getting angry—we feel wronged, after all—but there are all kinds of reasons for (eventually) letting it go. Even if our anger is righteous, perpetual anger is destructive—whether for its bearer or for society.

In our forum, philosopher Agnes Callard challenges this conventional view. Perhaps we shouldn't let our anger go. Our reasons for being angry are eternal, aren't they? No apology or redress ever erases the original injury that provoked the anger in the first place. "The affective response to injustice clings to the taste of blood," she writes. "Once you have a reason to be angry, you have a reason to be angry forever."

Reflecting on two millennia of debates about the value of anger, Callard contends that we have been asking the wrong question. The effort to distinguish righteous forms of anger from unjust vengeance, or appropriate responses to wrongdoing from inappropriate ones, is misguided. Maybe anger is not a bug of human life, but a feature—an emotion that, for all its troubling qualities, is an essential part of being a moral agent in an imperfect world. And if it is both troubling and essential, what, then, do we do with the implications that angry victims of injustice are themselves morally compromised, and that it might not be possible to respond rightly to being treated wrongly. Because anger cannot be morally pure, Callard draws the bracing conclusion: "We can't be good in a bad world."

The forum responses and essays that follow explore anger in its many forms—public and private, personal and political. With anger looming so large in our public life, these are issues we all must grapple with. Does the vast well of public anger compromise all of us?

ON
ANGER

Agnes Callard

Suppose that you are angry on Tuesday because I stole from you on Monday. Suppose that on Wednesday I return what I stole; I compensate you for any disadvantage occasioned by your not having had it for two days; I offer additional gifts to show my good will; I apologize for my theft as a moment of weakness; and, finally, I promise never to do it again. Suppose, in addition, that you believe my apology is sincere and that I will keep my promise.

Could it be rational for you to be just as angry on Thursday as you were on Tuesday? Moreover, could it be rational for you to conceive of a plan to steal from me in turn? And what if you don't stop at one theft: could it be rational for you to go on to steal from me again, and again, and again?

Though your initial anger at me might have been reasonable, we tend to view a policy of unending disproportionate revenge as paradigmatically irrational. Eventually we should move on, we are told, or let it go, or transmute our desire for revenge into a healthier or more respectable feeling. This idea has given rise to a debate among academic philosophers about the value of anger. Should we valorize it in terms of the righteous indignation of that initial response? Or should we vilify it in terms of the grudge-bearing vengeance of the unending one?

I am going to explain how that debate goes, but I am not going to try to resolve it. Instead, I am going to peel it away to reveal a secret that lies behind it: we have been debating the wrong issue. The real debate concerns the three questions about anger and rationality in my second paragraph, which are not rhetorical, and to which the answer might well be: yes, yes, and yes.

FIRST, the academic debate. In one corner, we have those who think that we would have a morally better world if we could eradicate anger entirely. This tradition has its roots in ancient Stoicism and Buddhism. The first-century Roman philosopher and statesman Seneca wrote that anger is a form of madness; he authored a whole treatise—*De Ira*, the title of this volume—about how to manage its ill effects. The eighth-century Indian philosopher and monk Śāntideva enjoined those wishing to travel the road of enlightenment to eliminate even the smallest seeds of anger, on the grounds that the full-blown emotion can only cause harm.

In the contemporary world, the philosopher Martha Nussbaum draws on Seneca and the Stoic tradition to argue that anger is an intrinsically mistaken attitude, since it is infected with a backward-looking "payback wish" that is vengeful and destructive. The correct response to any setback or injustice, in her view, is forward-looking: preventing similar events from occurring in the future. In a similar vein, Owen Flanagan, who draws on both Śāntideva's Buddhism and a Confucian-inflected metaphysics, sees anger as an intrinsically hostile attitude, one that falsely presupposes a self-centered metaphysics of individuals who possess "intentions to be cruel, and to do harm or evil."

In the other corner of the debate stand those who conceive of anger—up to a point—as an essential and valuable part of one's moral repertoire: anger is what sensitizes us to injustice and motivates us to uphold justice. By being angry with me on Tuesday, the day after I stole, you create the system and demand the terms under which I must acquiesce and "make things right" on Wednesday.

This pro-anger position has its roots in Aristotle's view that the (well-trained) passions are what allow the "eye of the soul" to perceive moral value, and finds its fullest expression in the British moral sentimentalists of the seventeenth and eighteenth centuries. The Earl of Shaftesbury, Frances Hutcheson, David Hume, and Adam Smith all held that our feelings are precisely what sensitize us to moral considerations.

Later, Peter Strawson's watershed paper "Freedom and Resentment" (1960) injected new life into the pro-anger cause by making emotions the fundamental mechanism of moral accountability.

Strawson develops Smith's insight that our status as moral creatures rests on the fact that we care—at an emotional level—what we think of one another. Strawson understands negative emotions in the anger family as paradigmatic expressions of moral assessment. Anger treats its target as someone capable of recognizing that she has done wrong and is to be contrasted with the indifference or calculating carefulness by which we might react to someone we see no hope of reintegrating into the moral community.

Strawson's continued influence is visible in the work of contemporary philosophers such as R. Jay Wallace, Jesse Prinz, Allan Gibbard, Pamela Hieronymi, and Jean Hampton. Though differing in their conclusions and many of the steps along the way, all begin from the sentimentalist assumption that emotions lie at the bottom of our practices of holding one another morally responsible. Emotions are how we humans do morality.

But are these two camps—the Stoics versus the sentimentalists—really diametrically opposed? Each must respond to the data that motivate the other, and when they do so, they make some surprising moves toward reconciliation.

Consider the data of the anti-anger side. There are at least two big drawbacks of anger, they note: first, the tendency to cling to one's anger, bearing a grudge deaf to any reasonable voice of reconciliation, apology, or restitution; second, the tendency to exact (often disproportionate) revenge. The fans of anger carve these phenomena off as pathologies, not essentially associated with anger. They use special words such as "indignation" and "resentment" to refer to anger purified of such impulses. Purified anger, they say, protests wrongdoing but is free of vengeful impulses and is immediately responsive to reasons to give up one's anger. (In this technical terminology, "resentment" is typically used to mark protesting on one's own behalf, whereas "indignation" is for protesting on behalf of another.) This move—carve away the dark side—is remarkably similar to the move the enemies of anger make when confronted with what we might call the "moral side" of anger.

Both Flanagan and Nussbaum, for instance, acknowledge that one who fails to react to grievous wrongdoing runs the risk of acquiescing in evil. They grant the importance of a moral sensibility that would lead a person to object to being treated with disrespect, but they hold that such a response is possible without anger proper. Flanagan uses the word "righteous indignation" to cover "judgment that such-and-such state of affairs is grievously wrong, the wrong ought to be righted, and a powerful emotional disposition to want to participate in righting the wrong without being angry." Nussbaum speaks of "transition anger," which is not so much anger as "quasi-anger": "the entire content of one's emotion is, 'How outrageous! Something must be done about this.'"

Notice what has happened: what started out as a battle over anger ends with everyone agreeing to avoid using that word. Instead, both sides prefer to segregate the "moral side" of anger (Tuesday's anger, which takes the form of rational and justified protest at injustice) from the "dark side" (Thursday's anger, which takes the form of irrational grudges and unjustifiable vengeance). It does not matter whether we follow the Strawsonians and call this moral side "indignation/resentment," or whether we use

Nussbaum and Flanagan's terminology of "transition anger" or "righteous indignation."

Now, when philosophers fail to disagree about any question of substance, you know someone is hiding something. In this case, I believe the pseudo-war has distracted us—and the combatants themselves—from the contentiousness of an assumption being made on all sides. Everyone assumes that we can retain the moral side of anger while distancing ourselves from paradigmatically irrational phenomena such as grudges and vengeance. But what if this is not the case? What if we humans do morality by way of vengeful grudges?

It is a fact of life that human beings have a direct emotional vulnerability to how we are treated, so when you wrong someone, you inflict on them the distinctive pain of unjust treatment. This moral sensibility on their part is included in the very meaning of what it is to "wrong someone": part of why wronging people is unjust is that they notice it.

It is also a fact of life that people tend to draw grudge-bearing and vengeful conclusions from premises involving genuinely moral facts about injustice and wrongdoing. I believe that we should not be too quick to pathologize this inference or dismiss it as a psychological tic. I will offer two arguments—the Argument for Grudges and the Argument for Revenge—that link those premises to those conclusions, suggesting that the reasoning in question is, in fact, valid. If we can't purify morality, we can't purify anger.

Callard

LET'S GO BACK to our original example. Is it rational for you to remain angry with me on Thursday, after all my hard work to restore justice? Both neo-Stoics such as Nussbaum and neo-sentimentalists such as Strawson would say no.

They would say that you ought to take into account how the wrongdoing that prompted your anger has been addressed, via restitution, compensation, apology, and a promise. I have made amends for my wrongdoing in every possible way; if you continue to be as angry as you were, it must be, they would argue, because you are being irrationally insensitive to those amends.

The tendency to cling to anger through apologies and recompense, for years sometimes and to the detriment of all parties concerned, is routinely dismissed as irrational. It is often supposed, specifically, that not "letting go" of one's anger must indicate a perverse pleasure in that anger. (Thus, poet Robert Burns in 1790: "Whare sits our sulky sullen dame / Gathering her brows like gathering storm / Nursing her wrath to keep it warm.")

But this idea ignores the fact that there are reasons to remain angry. And the reasons are not hard to find: they are the same reasons as the reasons to get angry in the first place. Apologies, restitution, and all the rest do nothing to cancel or alter the fact that I stole, nor the fact that I ought not to have stolen. Those facts were your reasons to be angry. Since they are not changed by my forms of redress—apology, compensation, what have you—then you still have, after the deployment of these amends, the very same reasons to be angry. Anger, after all, is not a desire to fix something but a way of grasping the fact that it is broken. You are angry about something that is now in the past, and there is nothing to be done about that. What I did will always diverge from what I ought to have done, no matter what I do *next*.

There are, of course, many nonrational ways your anger might come to an end: you could die, develop amnesia, or it could just fizzle out over time. Suppose one day, out of nowhere, you simply decide to set your anger aside, and you succeed. We might judge that decision to be in some sense "rational"—who wants to go through their whole life angry?—but not in the sense that your reason for anger has been addressed. It hasn't been, and it won't ever be. Once you have a reason to be angry, you have a reason to be angry forever. This is the Argument for Grudges.

Now for the Argument for Revenge. Your desire for revenge, like your holding a permanent grudge, is typically taken to be irrational and unjustified. But this conclusion is typically a product of the assumption that revenge aims to solve the problem of anger, once and for all, by balancing out or undoing the wrong done. Once we let go of this assumption that anger can be undone—you have a reason to be angry forever, after all—it is not hard to produce an argument in favor of revenge. We should not find this possibility surprising; it would be strange if one of the oldest and most universal human practices did not have a rationalizing explanation. The Argument for Revenge is simply that revenge is how we hold one another morally responsible.

When I steal from you, you see me as responsible for a serious gap between the way the world is and the way it ought to be; there is a perspectival opposition between us. You see my action as morally unacceptable, and you experience that unacceptability as a pain, a harm. But I, who did it, evidently saw it as a perfectly fine thing to do, having judged the action to be a good thing for me.

Assuming that I understood that what I was taking was yours, and that I was not acting under some kind of duress—ignorance and compulsion are mitigating factors—my theft indicates that I see the world in value-terms opposed to yours. Your "bad" is my "good." If you are to hold me accountable for this, instead of letting me off the hook, you will make this (accidental, adventitious) opposition a principle and rule for our interactions.

Revenge allows you to turn the principle of my action into a rule for your conduct toward me: you make my bad your good. This is the opposite of trying to undo or reverse my action. You hold me accountable by holding onto my theft, refusing to forget it, turning its one-off opposition between our interests into a rule to which I am now subject. You do not let me "live it down," instead you force my own thinking down my throat. Seeing me as accountable for what I have done means treating my action as a principle governing our interactions. Angry people sometimes describe their vengeance as "teaching someone a lesson," and this is quite literally true: you make my wronging of you into a general principle and then "educate" me by imposing it on me.

Educating me in this way is not easy on you: making my evil your good has psychological costs, among them the fact that you divert yourself away from what would otherwise be good for you. You must remodel your psychological landscape into one devoted to regulating mine. This explains the uncanny intimacy of anger: though you can't stand to be near me, it is also true that no one could be closer to you than me. I have infiltrated the patterns of your thought; I have my fingers on your heartstrings; I have even been put in charge of your sense perception: you see traces of me everywhere you look. You complain about me to anyone who will listen, and when no one will listen you shout at a mental effigy of me. I've colonized your fantasy life. Holding me responsible involves an embrace, albeit an adversarial one. Anger feels exactly as you would expect, if it were true that my moral accountability was a matter of your seeing what's good for you in terms of what's bad for me.

Again, as with grudges, the point is not that, all things considered, one should take revenge. One may take other factors besides anger into account in governing one's behavior. But insofar as one acts from anger, one pursues what is good for oneself by doing what is bad for another. This is perfectly rational, justified, and intelligible. Polemarchus, in Plato's *Republic*, expressed the hostile logic of anger: justice gives benefits to friends and harms to enemies.

These two arguments—the Argument for Grudges and the Argument for Revenge—suggest it is not so easy to separate the idea that anger is a moral sense from the thought that we should hold on to grudges, or to embrace anger as a mechanism of moral accountability without endorsing vengeance.

I do not claim that these arguments make an open-and-shut case; objections are certainly possible, and a full defense of the validity of these forms of reasoning would be a big project. My aim here has merely been to show that there is a case to be made for the conclusion that grudges and vengeance are perfectly rational—and that such a case is not an overly complicated one. The arguments I have offered are simple and intuitive, qualities that make their neglect in the philosophical debates—in the form of the unquestioned assumption, on both sides, that grudges and vengeance are irrational—all the more striking.

Striking, but not inexplicable. For if we put the two arguments together, the result is that someone who is angry never has a reason to sever the link between the other's evil and her own good. Perhaps the simple explanation for the neglect of these arguments is that we do not want to acknowledge the possibility that morally righteous anger provides rational grounds for limitless violence.

WHILE IT MAY SEEM, then, that the Stoics and sentimentalists are radically opposed, they share more than meets the eye. In particular, they share confidence—misplaced, I think—in a certain project of conceptual analysis. This project aims to identify a purified form of moral response, one incorporating all of the virtues and none of the vices of anger. I am not the first to argue that such a project is quixotic. Some version of my point can be found in a number of thinkers who approach questions of morality from a more historical and anthropological angle. Friedrich Nietzsche, Michel Foucault, and René Girard have all argued that the darkest sides of anger—vengeance, bloodlust, and limitless violence—are baked into the very idea of morality.

Nietzsche's *Genealogy of Morals* (1887) traces our present approach to morality to a turn away from a prehistorical ethic based on nobility and strength. The crucial sentiment guiding the new morality is ressentiment—a form of anger—felt by those previously oppressed and enslaved. What emerges is a "slave morality [that] from the outset says 'No' to what is 'outside,' what is 'different,' what is 'not itself'; and this 'No' is its creative deed." The negative or reactive morality we have ended up with foregrounds the concepts of guilt, conscience, promises, and duty. Nietzsche says these concepts are "soaked in blood thoroughly and for a long time. And might one not add that, fundamentally, this world has never since lost a certain odor of blood and torture?"

Girard's *Violence and the Sacred* (1972), a work of religious anthropology, discusses the role of human and animal sacrifice in the curbing of violence. Girard begins from the observation that every form of human community is threatened by one basic problem: once one act of violence happens, it threatens to set off a chain reaction of limitless retaliatory violence. According to Girard, what drives this chain reaction is nothing other than the moral horror at violence: "The obligation never to shed blood cannot be distinguished from the obligation to exact vengeance on those who shed it . . . it is precisely because they detest violence that men make a duty of vengeance." Girard's book contends that phenomena as widely varied as ancient scapegoating, Greek tragedy, and the sexual norms governing the nuclear family are all attempts to respond to this basic problem of the containment of violence.

Finally, Michel Foucault's *Discipline and Punish* (1975) analyzes the shift from punishment by public torture and execution to punishment by imprisonment. Foucault's thesis is that although these reforms were couched in the eighteenth-century language of human rights, their aim was to turn punishment into a focused attack on the prisoner's human rights: "From being an art of unbearable sensations, punishment has become an economy of suspended rights." Foucault then builds outward from the prison and argues that we can see the values of our society inscribed in the methodology of forcible restraint that characterizes such social artifacts as schools, examinations, timetables, and professional careers. The way we value freedom, autonomy, self-determination, and human rights is by taking those things away from people at every turn.

All three of these thinkers remain hugely influential despite having had the empirical details of their argumentation called into question by scholars from a variety of fields. I want to suggest that one reason for their enduring and even cult-like appeal is that they make a compelling and deep philosophical point that floats free of the particular historical-anthropological terms in which it is couched. What do these views have in common, after all? Nietzsche says we have built our whole morality out of resentful bloodlust; Girard says that violence and the opposition to violence are one; Foucault says that punishment is crime. The common denominator is the observation that human morality has a tendency to turn in on itself. Being a good person means, at times, being willing to do bad things.

I have offered reasons for thinking that the "dark side of morality" these three thinkers see mirrored in various social institutions derives ultimately from the logic of moral responsiveness: the morally correct way to respond to immorality is to do things—cling to anger, exact vengeance—that are in some way immoral.

If we abandon the anthropological distance and admit that we are the humans we are describing, grappling with this insight should produce nothing short of a crisis. We cannot climb outside of our own moral theory in order to assess it as bankrupt or broken; we must rely on it for the very terms of assessment. Of the three, Nietzsche comes the closest to facing this crisis, though even he often hides behind the suggestion that words such as "health" and "strength" offer him some kind of alternative footing. But who wants a society that is healthier or stronger unless those words are meant in a moralized sense—which is to say, a sense already shrouded by the darkness of our morality system? There is no magic trick that lets us climb outside our own normative skin.

ANGER IMPLICATES ALL OF US in moral corruption, then. Well, *almost* all of us. There is a certain Stoic so extreme that his position is represented by neither Nussbaum nor Flanagan, nor any modern thinker I know of. This Extreme Stoic sees emotions as having *no* role in morality; in order to achieve this complete emotional detachment, he places no value on anything the world can remove from himself, including his children, his life, and his freedom from physical torture. Extreme Stoics take inspiration from Socrates, who claimed that a good man could not be harmed, and who correspondingly denied that the Athenians were harming him when they put him to death for crimes he did not commit. Socrates died anger-free.

Most of us are neither willing nor able to achieve the kind of detachment that this immunity from wrath requires. When people commit injustice against us, we feel it: our blood boils. At that point, we have to decide how much we want to fight to quell our anger, how much effort we are going to put into repressing and suppressing that upswell of rage. The answer is rarely none. While we do not want to let our anger get away from us and drive us to its logical, eternally vengeful conclusion, if we quash it with too heavy a hand, we lose self-respect and, more generally, our moral footing. Inhibiting any and all anger in the face of genuine wrongdoing is acquiescing in evil. So, we are regularly faced with the complicated question of how much anger to permit ourselves under a given set of circumstances.

But notice that, if the arguments I have offered here are correct, this question is equivalent to asking: How much immorality should we permit ourselves? The realistic project of inhibiting anger must be distinguished from the idle fantasy of purifying it. We can use a word such as "indignation" or "transition anger" to postulate a feeling that righteously protests wrongdoing without any hint of eternality or vengeance—but the item to which that word refers is a philosopher's fiction. The multiplication of kinds and flavors and species and names for anger is designed to distract us from the crisis at the heart of anger, which is that affective response to injustice clings to the taste of blood.

I believe that, when faced with injustice, we should sometimes get somewhat angry. Such anger is not "pure" and entails submitting oneself to (some degree of) moral corruption, but the alternative, acquiescence, is often even worse. The point I want to emphasize, however, is this: just because the moral corruption of anger is our best option doesn't mean it is not corruption.

The consequences of acknowledging this point are sobering: victims of injustice are not as innocent as we would like to believe. Either these victims are morally compromised by the vengeful and grudge-bearing character of their anger, or they are morally compromised by acquiescence. Long-term oppression of a group of people amounts to long-term moral damage to that group. When it comes to racism, sexism, homophobia, anti-Semitism, ableism, classism, religious discrimination, anti-neurodiversity, elitism of any stripe, this argument entails that the oppressors have made the oppressed morally worse people. Of course, oppressing people is also bad for your soul, but we do not need to be reminded of *that*; we are accustomed to the thought that wronging others makes you a bad person. My point is: so does being wronged, even if to a lesser degree.

I moved to the United States from Hungary when I was five years old, but I still spent my childhood summers there, at Lake Balaton. Across the street from my grandparents' house there was a resort popular among East Germans. I could not enter the resort area—it was surrounded by a fence—but one summer, when I was around ten years old, I befriended a girl around my age who was vacationing there. We had no common language, but we communicated by way of a marching game: we played soldiers and invented a complicated militaristic dance to which we would add moves day by day. We marched side by side, separated by the fence—until the day I was caught by my grandmother.

My grandmother was a concentration camp survivor, so she was horrified by what she saw: her granddaughter, marching with one of Them. I tried to explain that we were only playing a game, but to her it was clear: I was collaborating with the enemy. I argued that her prejudice against the German girl was no different from the Germans' prejudice against us. My protest only made her angrier, and I was forbidden from ever approaching the girl again.

But how innocent was my game, really? All four of my grandparents, in fact, had survived concentration camps; all of them lost almost everyone they knew in the Holocaust. My grandmother denied that the Holocaust was the greatest tragedy of her life, giving that honor to the fact that her first child, my uncle, was born with cerebral palsy. But she even blamed that on the Nazis, perhaps not without reason: there are many stories of birth injury in the first generation of children born to women who had suffered malnutrition and other forms of abuse in concentration camps. (My other grandmother's first baby was stillborn.)

My parents decided to leave Hungary when the synagogue on our block was blown up. (After that, the Jews in the area went to my grandmother's house to pray, secretly.) When we arrived in New York City, my parents pulled me out of public school after I was beaten up for wearing a necklace with a Star of David. They could not afford private school, but Orthodox Jewish elementary schools were willing to accept my sister and me for free, as charity cases. Why? Because the Holocaust, of course—which, at those schools, was its own subject, alongside English, math, and science. Before high school, I hardly wrote a poem or short story that was *not* in some way about the Holocaust.

Anti-anti-Semitism was so much the theme of my childhood that it is simply impossible to believe I accidentally fell into playing soldiers with a German girl. I wasn't innocent. But my grandmother wasn't innocent, either: she was full of anger. Innocence was not a possibility.

NIETZSCHE, FOUCAULT, AND GIRARD contributed to a strand of cultural criticism often invoked in support of attitudes of cynicism, misanthropy, and pessimism about the human condition. They are seen as radicals. In my view, however, all three are to be faulted for their timidity. It is striking the degree to which each writer held himself at a safe anthropological distance from the dark side of morality he so accurately described. If they had stepped inside their own theories, they would have immediately drawn the simple, devastating conclusion that it is impossible for humans—you and me and the three of them included—to respond rightly to being treated wrongly. We can't be good in a bad world.

Callard

FORUM
RESPON

FORUM RESPONSES

CHOOSING VIOLENCE
Paul Bloom

IN THE SIXTH SEASON of HBO's *Game of Thrones*, Lancel Lannister demands that Cersei appear before the High Sparrow. She refuses. When a soldier steps forward to take her by force, her enormous bodyguard, the Mountain, intervenes. "Order your man to step aside," Lancel says, "or there will be violence." There is a long beat. At last Cersei responds, softly, "I choose violence."

Agnes Callard chooses violence as well. She defends the value of "vengeance, bloodlust, and limitless violence." For her, this is what morality is all about. Violence is the cost we pay for goodness.

I think she is right; indeed, hers is the received view in evolutionary approaches to the mind. No serious scholar sees anger as a glitch or an accident. Like every other complex cognitive system, it evolved through natural selection and serves a biological function: it motivates us to defend the interests both of ourselves and of those we care for. Any social creature that wasn't inclined to strike back at threats or acts of harm would be, in a word, a chump—open to exploitation and cruelty, a loser at survival and reproduction. There is now abundant evidence that punitive impulses are universal in humans, present in young children, and bred in the bone.

This is part of what makes human society possible. Humans are unusual among primates: hundreds of people who have never met can share a ride on an airplane for several hours, say, emerging with all their fingers and toes still attached. As the primatologist Sarah Hrdy points out, the outcome would be very different for a planeload of unacquainted chimps. It is likely that the difference stems from our capacity and inclination for retaliation. We control our violent impulses because we know that others won't let us get away with them. Ironically, then, what might make our species more social than even our closest evolutionary relatives is that we are more easily pissed off.

Callard is thus on the right track when she speculates, "What if we humans do morality by way of vengeful grudges?" She comes to her conclusion not by way of evolution or game theory, of course, but rather through philosophical reflection and a close reading of Nietzsche, Foucault, and Girard. But this is a pleasing convergence: when people arrive at the same idea from different directions, there is good reason to believe that the idea is right.

So far so good. I am puzzled by another feature of Callard's argument, though: her repeated claim that being angry isn't *just* natural, or universal, or essential to morality—more than that, she says it is *rational*. It is not that I disagree; I don't understand what she means.

When we talk about rationality, we often refer to reasoning: drawing conclusions in accordance with the laws of logic. If you think that Socrates is a man and all men are mortal, then it is rational to believe that Socrates is mortal. Sometimes we also talk about not just beliefs but actions as being rational, when they are properly suited to one's goals. If it is raining outside and you don't want to get wet, it is rational to carry an umbrella. But I am not sure how any of this extends to feelings. If my partner flirts with someone, is it rational for me to get jealous? Is it rational to be cheered by a sunny day, disgusted at certain sex acts, bored at a faculty meeting, bitter at the success of an enemy? It doesn't seem that normal standards of rationality apply here.

Now, if by "rational," Callard means "working as these systems have evolved to work," then there is no problem. But some of Callard's examples aren't consistent with this interpretation. She suggests that anger is a way of grasping that something has gone wrong in the past and reasons that, since the past doesn't change, it follows that, "Once you have a reason to be angry, you have a reason to be angry forever." But anger isn't *just* an acknowledgment of a state of affairs; it is also, as Callard herself emphasizes, a motivational state, connected to a desire for vengeance. So, yes, it is rational for me to appreciate that even a tiny wrong never goes away, but this isn't the same as saying that it is rational for me to want to enact vengeance for it many years later. It probably isn't.

More generally, it is not clear how Callard's analysis bears on the question of whether the role anger plays in morality can change over time. It could be that anger was once necessary for the emergence of morality but is obsolete now. After all, a child who learns to count using her fingers will turn into an adult who can count just fine with her hands in her pockets. Or, more plausibly, it could be that some amount of anger is needed for morality to continue to work, but this amount is less, perhaps much less, than we have now.

This last claim is an empirical one, and we have quite a lot of data that bear on it. With the exception of those with severe brain damage, every normal human feels anger. But there is plenty of variation, across individuals as well as societies, in how it is experienced and expressed. Do the easily angered lead better lives than those who are quick to forgive? Do angry people make the best romantic partners? Are cultures of honor, in which male violence against transgressors is a core moral value, the best societies to live in? I think the answer to all of these questions is no, and I wonder whether Callard agrees.

"Emotions are how we humans do morality," Callard tells us, and this is true—but emotions are not *the only way* we do morality. There are those who meditate to reduce their anger; there are those who think retributive punishment is rooted in a metaphysical confusion; there are Stoics and Buddhists and utilitarians. Callard is perhaps right that our judgments are inevitably "shrouded by the darkness of our morality system." But, still, we can argue about morality, revise and defend and extend and challenge our initial prejudices. This too is how humans do morality. After all, what else are we up to right now?

THE KINGDOM OF DAMAGE
Elizabeth Bruenig

WHEN MY HUSBAND was in law school, he used to relate to me every-thing he was learning as a kind of memory exercise. I would typically pose a few naive questions. One evening he raised the matter of torts, and the ways a liable wrongdoer might redress the harm they've done. Almost always, I noticed, the restitution was monetary, even where the harm hadn't been. "Why money?" I asked, not expecting much more than the idea that money is a universal solvent. Instead my husband dashed off a theory I've been considering since. As far as the law is concerned, when you harm someone, a piece of property is created—their damage, so to speak—and you, the wrongdoer, must buy it from the victim to satisfy (or at least exhaust) their claim against you.

Though I may have intuited it before, I had never quite realized so distinctly that harms can't actually be redressed. Whatever you lose when someone hurts you, you lose for good; whatever they supply to make amends can never return you to your prior state of having never been hurt. For the law, this is a problem—because, as Agnes Callard points out, it means that the wronged have an eternal warrant for vengeance, and pose a permanent threat to peace. The imaginary property dreamed into being by tort law provides a remedy by way of metaphor. Once you surrender your damage for recompense, you have no further claim to it. So it goes with property.

But the metaphor was illuminating in other ways, too. In some sense, our damage is our own kingdom: an interior place of pain and outrage but also moral clarity, where we know that, in being angry over having been wronged, we are in the right. This picture adds a dose of concreteness to our talk of "dwelling on" aggrievement. Not only are people logically entitled to interminable anger over harm done—they have compelling emotional and moral reasons to hang onto a grudge.

This is a problem for us humans. We're pathologically inclined to hurt one another, but also inherently in need of society. The infinite prosecution of grievances is arguably justifiable, but it is also certainly apocalyptic. We cannot all be like Michael Kohlhaas—protagonist of the eponymous, early nineteenth-century novella by the German novelist Heinrich von Kleist—pressing our rightful claims to vengeance and recompense until our demands dissolve all the bonds around us, eventually destroying us. The righteousness of Kohlhaas is a form of justice society cannot withstand.

Law may have its makeshift remedy to this conundrum in its figurative property sales, but what of morality? Callard argues that the wronged have no rational reason to forgo their anger, and by this I gather she means that there is no obvious benefit to the aggrieved in releasing their contempt. Surrendering their damage, so to speak, doesn't remedy what was done to them; neither does it ensure that such a thing won't happen again, nor does it impart useful moral lessons for the wrongdoer. Worse, it doesn't even generally feel good.

What Callard has identified is the fact that forgiveness is unfair and painful. Much is made of the healing power of forgiveness, but in my experience, this therapeutic promise falls somewhere between being overstated and totally empty. Forgiving someone for hurting you is excruciating, because it requires you to follow an unjust wrong with a personal sacrifice. And yet: forgiveness is also good, and it may be a necessary ingredient for peace as we know it.

Whatever else forgiveness is or entails, it certainly requires giving up further claims to punitive action against a wrongdoer. It does not require that the wronged party seek no redress, only that the redress be limited. Neither does it require that the wronged party give up all traces of anger toward the wrongdoer, only that the anger cease to be acted on, and perhaps fade over time. Anger as a sentiment can remain, but forgiveness as a moral discipline transforms that anger into a less socially corrosive substance.

This isn't to say that societies *must* advise forgiveness if they mean to remain intact. As classicist David Konstan observes in his book *Before Forgiveness: The Origins of a Moral Idea* (2010), Greek and Roman cultures of antiquity got along all right without forgiveness as we understand it. In their worlds, Konstan writes, "the appeasement of anger and the relinquishing of revenge were . . . perceived as resting on the restoration of the dignity of the injured party, whether through compensation or gestures of deference, or else by way of discounting the offense on the grounds that it was in some sense involuntary or unintentional."

We still retain this tendency to avoid the sting of forgiveness by retroactively obliterating the bad act itself—that is, by explaining why the initial wrong isn't something one can be justifiably angry about because it was somehow unintentional. Yet we're also less comfortable than the Greeks or Romans were with compulsory displays of deference—say, public self-abasement, as in begging and pleading for pardon, prostrating oneself, or pledging service to one's erstwhile victim.

Konstan argues that our contemporary version of forgiveness is a Christian-infused outgrowth of the Enlightenment, specifically the Kantian exhortation to treat all people as ends, not means. That maxim envisions a baseline moral equality that the Greeks and Romans rejected. Indeed, it appears that societies can survive sans forgiveness, but not the sort of society we want to have. In a putatively liberal-democratic order, we would prefer that our peace not be based upon enforcing a rigid social hierarchy; we must allow wrongdoers to reclaim a moral status equal to that of their victims, somehow, in order for an egalitarian polity to have any hope of enduring. Otherwise, the thoroughly inegalitarian futures Callard warns of might ensue. While oppressors might be morally degraded by their decision to oppress, so, too, would the oppressed, by their entanglement in limitless vengeance.

Forgiveness thus seems to be a crucial component of maintaining our preferred social order. But that doesn't mean it is a therapeutic or self-serving one. In its capacity to halt an otherwise endless campaign of vengeance, forgiveness echoes René Girard's definition of sacrifice in *Violence and the Sacred* (1972): an expression of limited violence which, when discharged, puts an end to the acceleration and reciprocation of violence. Unlike human, animal, or even token sacrifices, forgiveness requires only the destruction of that sacred property—one's own damage, the interior realm of righteous pain, that wellspring of anger.

It is a mistake to frame forgiveness as something one does for oneself, as pop psychologists and wellness coaches often do. A forgiver might experience some benefits in the act of forgiveness, but it is just as likely that they will experience a secondary wave of pain. After all, they, the innocent, are being asked to sacrifice for some higher good: peace or egalitarian order, in the modern formulation, God in a more archaic version. And yet this strange custom—contrary to an individualist, ruthlessly rights-oriented point of view as it is—may well be the thin membrane separating our (aspirational) way of life from more violent, less egalitarian forms. And thus we may all be obligated to practice it.

ANGER AND THE POLITICS
OF THE OPPRESSED
Desmond Jagmohan

WHILE ANGER IS A COMPLEX EMOTION that has both cognitive and visceral properties, philosophers have long argued that there are morally right and morally wrong ways for us to express our anger. As Agnes Callard outlines, most philosophers view anger as a moral response to injustice while a smaller camp, stemming from the Stoic tradition, consider the emotion a wellspring for spite. Martha Nussbaum, for example, worries that anger often leads to narcissism and vindictiveness —behavior bent on "payback." Malpractice and divorce litigation are among her favorite examples of such moral conceits: a retributive attitude that revives neither life nor love.

Though Nussbaum says a lot about anger in private life, she seems primarily interested in its place in politics, especially in contexts of persecution. In *Anger and Forgiveness* (2016), she concedes that anger can be a valuable political emotion: when the oppressed get angry, it signals that they recognize the wrong done to them. Anger can also motivate protests of such wrongs. Still, in response to retaliatory rage, Nussbaum argues for transitional anger, a mental pivot away from seeking payback to "more productive forward-looking thoughts, asking what can actually be done to increase either personal or social welfare."

Nussbaum thus focuses on how anger shapes social action rather than on angry feelings. She concentrates, for example, on conditions that were ripe for retaliatory anger—colonization, Jim Crow, and apartheid—but in which an oppressive regime fell to a politics that transcended anger and resentment. For Nussbaum, Mohandas Gandhi, Martin Luther King, Jr., and Nelson Mandela paved a revolutionary path when they expressed and mobilized anger the morally right way. But, as Callard warns, this is part of a larger attempt to isolate anger's admirable qualities from its "darker side." Callard says we should face the fact that the morally correct response to oppression may require us to act immorally. I agree.

Still, I fear that both Nussbaum and Callard offer quite narrow views of the moral life of the oppressed. Nussbaum holds up noble saints while Callard naturalizes violence when she points to René Girard. I agree with Callard when she says victims can be morally *compromised* by the anger they feel in response to their oppression or by their acquiescence to such conditions. But I part ways with her when she says enduring oppression leaves victims morally *damaged*. It is difficult for me to imagine the black men and women who faced down Bull Connor and his henchmen at the Edmund Pettus Bridge as morally diminished; it is also difficult for me to imagine the black men and women who did not march that day as ethically broken. But it is not difficult for me to imagine racist and moderate whites that sustained that world as morally shattered souls. We seem to ask a lot more of the oppressed than we do of oppressors.

An implicit but foundational assumption is that people owe it to their self-respect to get angry in the face of oppression and to express their anger to others. That is to say failing to protest injustice vitiates self-respect. Nussbaum, to her credit, questions this view. Callard, on the other hand, insists of anger that "if we quash it with too heavy a hand, we lose self-respect and, more generally, our moral footing." In the realm of politics, appearances are what really matter. Normative judgments about a person's self-respect are almost always based on how he or she appears before us.

For many, silence in the face of injustice reveals a morally damaged character. This assumption prevails in discussions of protest against racial injustice. Thomas Hill, Jr., and Bernard Boxill, for example, argue that self-respect requires protesting the wrong done to you and communicating to the public your resistance to the moral injury you suffer. A favorite example of Hill's is the *servile slave*. His deference and fawning conveys to others that he accepts the idea that blacks are inferior, that he thinks they are owed less than whites, and makes visible his damaged self-respect. For Boxill, it therefore follows that protest is a prima facie duty; expressing anger at your subjugation affirms your dignity, even when it does not reform society or aggravates your condition. These judgments assume the servile slave is not a prudent calculator, that his compliance discloses his true feelings. Tommie Shelby amends this view when he says self-respect requires resistance, but it does not oblige a subjugated person to protest—that is, to make public her anger. Concealing her resistance can preserve her self-respect.

To better understand the difficulty in accurately judging the visible behavior of those living under oppression, let us consider two scenes from Frederick Douglass's second autobiography, *My Bondage and My Freedom* (1855). The first passage is rather famous. Those who view self-respect as requiring protest frequently point to Douglass's fight with the slave-breaker Covey. The "battle with Mr. Covey," wrote Douglass, "was the turning point in my '*life as a slave*'. . . . It recalled to life my crushed self-respect, and my self-confidence, and inspired me with a renewed determination to be a *free man*. A man, without force, is without the essential dignity of humanity." Douglass's fury at slavery inspired his revolt, which proved morally restorative but politically ineffectual. His moral resurrection did not change his status as a slave. He remained the property of another.

Later in the narrative, Douglass said his master, Hugh Auld, permitted him to work as a caulker in the shipyards so long as he gave all of his earnings to Auld. Though pivotal to Douglass's emancipation, this second scene attracts far less commentary. "I could see no reason," Douglass railed, "why I should, at the end of each week, pour the reward of my honest toil into the purse of any man. The thought itself vexed me." His master's robbery was akin to Covey's brutality. But if he openly resisted, his master would sell him into the Deep South, thus making escape impossible. Escaping slavery required that he remain on Maryland's eastern shore so he could work and siphon some of his wages. So, Douglass submitted to his master's wishes.

But the taking of his earnings "kept the nature and character of slavery constantly" before him, assuring that his deceit never slipped into self-deception. That is to say, Douglass donned a mask of compliance to conceal his seditious intentions:

> It is a blessed thing that the tyrant may not always know the thoughts and purposes of his victim. Master Hugh little knew what my plans were. . . . My object, therefore, in working steadily, was to remove suspicion, and in this I succeeded admirably. He probably thought I was never better satisfied with my condition, than at the very time I was planning my escape.

Imagine, for a moment, you witnessed the first scene without knowing Douglass's inner thoughts or motives. You would likely conclude that he revolted because he abhorred the injustice of slavery, and though he remained a slave he salvaged his self-respect. Now imagine witnessing the second scene without Douglass's account of his motives. All you see is a slave laboring and, without a trace of anger or resentment, handing over his wages to his master. You would probably conclude that Douglass is Hill's *servile slave*, someone whose acquiescence to oppression vitiates his self-respect.

The point is that those who are most oppressed have the most compelling reasons to be angry. They also have the most compelling reasons to never express their anger publicly. In the Jim Crow South, a slip of the tongue or a misplaced glance could get you killed. Often it was cunning, not confrontation, that made possible effective resistance. We should therefore avoid making strong normative judgments about people who seem to succumb to their domination. We have no way of knowing whether the lack of anger an undocumented immigrant expresses when cooking our food, cleaning our home, and sustaining our entire economy is sincere or a strategic response to her exploitation and oppression. The absence of resentment and rage in her words and deeds says nothing about her self-respect.

Despite Nussbaum's reservations, it is rational for an undocumented worker to be angry and vengeful at a society that exploits her labor while denying her basic rights and protections. But the risk of further persecution might submerge her outrage beneath compliant smiles. She likely reasons that our uncertainty about her sense of self-respect is not worth her doing something that lands her and her children in cages. Maybe we should strive harder to think with the oppressed rather than to think for them. Doing so will require us to offer more than impossible models of political morality or veiled nihilism.

THE SOCIAL LIFE OF ANGER

Daryl Cameron & Victoria Spring

AGNES CALLARD DECONSTRUCTS arguments about the "dark side" of anger as a social emotion. While she agrees with critics that anger can motivate grudge-holding and punishment, she shifts the conversation by suggesting these are moral features of anger, not bugs. Some philosophers suggest anger's perseverance and link to vengeance mean anger should be dismissed as a moral guide, unless it can be somehow "purified." Callard suggests this may not be possible, or even morally desirable.

We agree with much of Callard's argument, which echoes ongoing debates in psychology about the dark sides of emotions such as outrage. Outrage—anger at moral transgressions—has been criticized for seeming to foster viral mob behavior online. Yet as Callard notes, anger can provide useful information about the world. Many scholars in affective science would agree that emotions can be rational guides. Indeed, we have argued against the tendency to vilify emotions such as outrage and empathy, because such interpretations overlook important social functions of these emotions. Focusing on anger's "impurities" may be the wrong approach. Instead, we might ask, why do people choose to engage with their anger or not?

Callard's first point is about grudges. Anger is thought to be problematic because it motivates unending grudges, even after attempts to repair the relationship, but Callard questions whether this is irrational: "once you have a reason to be angry, you have a reason to be angry forever." She acknowledges that one might decide to "set one's anger aside"—a process that may occur through emotion regulation. Anger can be a rational response to the environment while still allowing that someone's perspective on the reason for the anger, and their judgment of how important that transgression is to the relationship, might change.

Indeed, research on emotion regulation finds that people can change their emotions by altering how they think about the world. New information might change how people think about transgressions and perpetrators, which can in turn reduce anger. It may or may not be rational to update a prior belief about the world, and this will likely vary by context. This shifts the conversation from whether anger has invariable consequences to why and how people choose to engage with their emotions in different ways. People vary in their motives to regulate their feelings, anger included. There are many ways to deal with anger; people could choose to maintain it, amplify it, or diminish it, and whether these are rational strategies depends on a person's goals, which may or may not include the goal of acknowledging the original harm done by the perpetrator.

Sustaining anger indefinitely may carry its own costs. Anger, like any emotion, might be exhausting to experience. Others have brought up the prospect of "outrage fatigue," or the dilution of anger by experiencing it for too long. This feels particularly relevant to the argument put forth by Callard. If one is entitled to feel anger infinitely, does that put one at greater risk for outrage fatigue and therefore make one more likely to let anger dissipate or fail to exert moral action? If an actor's anger becomes fatiguing, and they fail to assert a demand for justice, do they feel immoral for allowing the transgression to go unpunished? And does anger even become tiring at all? To us, these are fascinating psychological questions that warrant more study.

This brings us to Callard's second point about revenge. She suggests that when someone has wronged you, it changes your fundamental relationship with that person. One of the more compelling features of this argument is the idea that being wronged carries psychological costs for the self; it forces you to "remodel your psychological landscape" to focus on managing the other person. In our own work, we have examined emotions such as outrage and empathy from a motivated emotion regulation perspective—understanding how people relate to their emotions in different ways depending on the perceived costs and benefits of these emotions. The cost of remodeling a moral relationship has been less well studied, particularly for decisions about maintaining or reducing anger. According to one theory of moral judgment, much of morality is about regulating relationships, deciding what kind of relationship model you have with another person and whether they've violated its implicit norms. We agree with Callard that moral transgressions may alter the relationship model you have with someone, and that this could introduce its own costs; however, we suggest that more work be done to understand how people might choose to flexibly apply different relationship models to deal with transgressors.

We also agree with Callard that it is important not to overlook the functions of anger. By treating moralistic punishment as a key feature of anger, not a problem, Callard's argument is consistent with a body of research on the role of anger in motivating moralizing behaviors (e.g., costly punishment) and collective action (e.g., volunteering or protesting). Even if people disagree about the right types of punishment or the right ways to vote, there may be more consensus in the notion that it is important for people to want to maintain moral order and express civic voice. The link between outrage (and, by extension, anger) and collective action might be important to consider, particularly for groups at a structural disadvantage. Callard rightly notes that anger could be disruptive and that attempts to delegitimize anger could even undermine its moral function.

Indeed, Callard addresses the disproportionate impact that oppression—and anger experienced over oppression—has on minoritized group members. "Victims of injustice," she writes, "are not as innocent as we would like to believe. Either these victims are morally compromised by the vengeful and grudge-bearing character of their anger, or they are morally compromised by acquiescence." We appreciate Callard's argument here. An additional consideration that we have previously discussed in the context of outrage concerns which groups are *allowed* to experience anger. Although members of minority groups are justified in being angry about their oppression, members of the majority group sometimes vilify them for that anger—as if the mere experience of anger is fundamentally immoral and violent.

The choice presented by Callard at the end of her essay is an important one. Do you mute your anger and risk seeming to acquiescence to the transgression, or do you respond with anger and risk engaging in behaviors that might be problematic in their own right? These choices may become especially complex when others challenge whether you are allowed to express anger in the first place. To move the debate forward, we suggest there be more scientific study and ethical discussion about the motivations, beliefs, and values that inform how people act on their anger.

Cameron & Spring

MORE IMPORTANT THINGS
Myisha Cherry

IN THE SPRING of 1961, Princeton University historian Eric Goldman hosted James Baldwin, C. Eric Lincoln, George Schuyler, and
Malcolm X on an episode of NBC's public affairs show *The Open
Mind*. Although the topic was civil rights more generally, the panel-
ists focused on the Nation of Islam. As Nicholas Buccola's new book
The Fire Upon Us (2019) highlights, Goldman appeared to frustrate
and exasperate Baldwin, as he sought "to find out . . . whether the
Muslim movement does hate me or not, and whether it proposes to
use force to satisfy that hatred." While he expressed some criticism
of the Nation of Islam's approach to resistance, Baldwin thought
these were the wrong questions.

Instead, Baldwin asked whether whites were ready to face up to
"the crimes for which they are responsible." Rather than evaluating
black folks' emotions and attitudes, Baldwin believed it was more
important to examine the context that gave birth to them. He continued this same line of reasoning throughout his writings. When civil

rights activist Medgar Evers was assassinated, for example, Baldwin was not interested in examining the evils in the heart of the killer; instead, in *Nothing Personal* (1964), Baldwin asked how the United States had, as Buccola puts it, "created a virulent atmosphere of hatred."

The same Baldwinian criticism might be leveled at the inquiry underlying the debate about anger and rationality. Consider this way of formulating the questions Callard begins with:

> After becoming a victim of racial discrimination, could it be rational for you to be just as angry on Thursday as you were on Tuesday, for my denying you a job on Monday based on your race? Moreover, could it be rational for you to conceive of a plan to ensure that I lose my job? And what if you don't stop at me losing my current job: could it be rational for you to go on to make sure that I never work for a public service organization again?

These are interesting philosophical questions, but are they the *most important* ones? Should they come at the expense of asking other questions, like: Are whites willing to own up to the fact that they have created an environment in which racial minorities are discriminated against? Baldwin would probably say no—these questions should not be sidelined.

This is not to say that certain questions about the logical structure of the ethics of anger cannot be asked. Nonetheless, if we start and end there—as if they are the most important—we fail to ask more relevant ones, ones that address *causes* instead of mere *symptoms*. And it is the relevant questions that help us resist the alluring tendency to promote racial mythologies, to pathologize

Cherry

and victim-blame, and to allow the racial sources of anger remain hidden and go unchallenged.

Some philosophers who follow this Baldwinian reasoning hail from the feminist tradition. Their method of inquiry focuses on an analysis of the social context from which anger arises, although they do not omit questions concerning the rationality of anger. Making sense of the context was, perhaps, the most important step to correcting or curing the social problem—for how could one come up with effective tools to combat injustice without a proper diagnosis of the injustice in the first place?

For example, poet and essayist Audre Lorde proudly claimed anger as an appropriate response to racism: "We operate in the teeth of a system for whom racism and sexism are primary, established, and necessary props of profit." And to those who thought her anger was too harsh, Lorde responded, "is it my manner that keeps her from hearing, or the message that her life may change?" The work of Marilyn Frye offers another example. Rather than just defend the rationality of anger of black women to others, Frye also gives an account of what limits a white man's capacity to comprehend and give uptake to a black woman's anger.

After these philosophers raise the relevant questions, they undergo a project to reclaim anger—an emotion they believe could combat the racist and sexist context that gave rise to it. Macalester Bell, for example, writes that while we tend to center anger's instrumental uses, anger at racial injustice also has intrinsic value: it shows a love for virtue and hatred for vice. Alison Jagger claims that in a capitalist, white-supremacist, and patriarchal society, minorities will be expected to express emotions such as joy rather than blameworthy, "outlaw" emotions such as anger that transgress affective norms. And Amia Srinivasan argues that even if anger at racial injustice is counterproductive, it is still appropriate.

Are these anger reclaimers—like the Stoic and Aristotelian camps—guilty of what Callard calls the desire to "segregate 'the moral side' of anger . . . from the 'dark side'"? I do not think they are. For example, while Lisa Tessman admits that "unrelenting anger or rage . . . may help the politically resistant self-pursue liberatory aims," she adds that this may come at the price of "being corrosive to the self" and having to "maintain painful, corrosive, extremely taxing, or self-sacrificial character traits." A particular kind of anger at racial injustice is necessary in anti-racist struggle—I refer to it as *Lordean rage*—but that does not mean anger cannot go wrong. Even though its target, action tendency, and aims are quite different from those of more destructive kinds of anger (e.g., narcissistic and white rage), Lordean rage is not by definition virtuous. These examples show that it is possible to defend anger by highlighting both its moral and dark side.

Callard concludes that "victims of injustice are not as innocent as we would like to believe." But, again, I do not think innocence is the right thing to be concerned with here. Neither do I think that those outraged at racial injustice are as concerned with innocence as some might think.

First, members of the dominant group are often thought to be innocent in their anger, but racial minorities are not. For example, Baldwin's Cambridge debate foe, William Buckley, had empathy and compassion for the rage of racist white southerners, but described Baldwin as a "tormented Negro writer . . . who celebrates his bitterness against the white community."

Second, we miss the point of anger at racial injustice if we think innocence has a certain moral and political weight. Being angry at injustice is about coming to grips with our past and our future. The anger is used to ensure we pursue and prevent racial injustice, express the value of victims of oppression, challenge a racialized system, and demand a better way. This anger is not about innocence, nor does its success depend on it.

As Buccola notes, the virtues that Baldwin considered essential to freedom include charity, intelligence, resilience, and spiritual force. Innocence does not make the cut. I concede that those who are angry at racial injustice are both corrupt and wounded. I am not surprised by this, though. Instead I am grateful that there exist corrupt and wounded folk who are willing to use their anger at racial injustice to make the world better—not in the absence of these traits, but in spite of them.

This gives me *less* reason to think that judging their rationality is such an important endeavor. And it gives me *more* reason to think that I am not worthy to rub accusations of non-innocence in their faces on Tuesday, Thursday, or any day of the week.

HOW ANGER GOES WRONG

Jesse Prinz

ANGER HAS GOTTEN a bad rap. It is condemned by the world's religions and in many philosophical traditions; we'd be better off ridding ourselves of rage, they say, and condemning fury to the flames. Agnes Callard has, heroically, come to anger's defense, presenting it as a necessary evil in an imperfect world. She goes further, suggesting that it is rational to crave revenge, and she rejects efforts to distinguish toxic anger from righteous indignation. Yet her embrace of this embattled emotion may go too far. We have much to learn by reflecting on what anger is good for and where it may err.

Critiques of anger abound. In the Bhagavad Gītā, Krishna describes anger as among our greatest enemies, which can lead only to delusion and despair. Buddhism counts anger as one of the three mental poisons, or *kleshas*; in Tibetan depictions of the Wheel of Life, anger is personified as a snake at the very center of the wheel, which, along with a bird (attachment) and a pig (ignorance), causes the unenlightened masses to remain trapped in a cycle of endless rebirth. The seminal Confucian philosopher, Xunzi, warns that rage will cause one to perish, and he says that we should learn to punish crime without anger. Zhuangzi, one of Taoism's greatest luminaries, advises each of us to drift through life like an empty boat, to avoid incurring anyone's rage. The Hebrew Bible depicts God as wrathful but cautions against human anger. Psalm 37, for example, urges that we forgo rage toward evildoers and trust the Lord to mete out justice. Christianity places emphasis on love and mercy, and the Holy Quran repeatedly refers to Allah as forgiving and forbearing.

Like Callard, I find such injunctions unsettling, in part because they can be used as a form of social control. Hinduism discourages anger while also encouraging the underclasses to accept their lot—what seems like a recipe for complacency. Ashoka the Great promoted the spread of Buddhism only after authorizing violent conquests, in a move that might cynically be interpreted as an attempt to pacify vengeful sentiments among the vanquished. Taoist injunctions against anger sometimes imply that we should be silent in the face of injustice, and Nietzsche argues that Christian love conceals a deep hatred of life-affirming values and makes virtues of weakness and mindless obedience.

Behind these worries lies the recognition that anger can be an instrument of liberation. It can stir those who have been oppressed to rise up against injustice. It can motivate rebellions against tyranny and fights for civil rights. We've seen anger put to powerful use in the Me Too movement, and it is a rallying call that brings people to the polls and to the streets.

Anger has subtler benefits as well. For example, the contemporary philosopher Céline Leboeuf observes that anger can mitigate the withering effects of racism. The white gaze can lead people of color to feel unwelcome, incompetent, criminalized, sexualized, dehumanized, or otherwise degraded. Anger, Leboeuf argues, can restore a sense dignity. It can also play a therapeutic role, as when we delight in stories of vengeance.

In fact, anger is even more than a rallying cry and symbolic balm. It may also be a necessary component of morality. According to the "sentimentalist" tradition in moral philosophy, morality is not a feature of the objective world, to be discovered like scientific facts, but rather a product of human preferences. Like deliciousness and beauty, it is not inherent in things out there, but rather in how these things impact us. A world without anger is a world where nothing is wrong. Without it, we would be like asteroids colliding indifferently in space. Indignation distinguishes assault from mere impact. We cannot relinquish anger without losing our moral sense.

FROM ALL THIS it does not follow, however, that all anger is good. Here we must turn back to Callard's complaint against those who try to distinguish bad anger from righteous indignation. She sees this as a hopeless cause, noting that anger's dark side—the thirst for retribution—is an inevitable part of the package. I too think we should not turn off the urge to get even; anger so inoculated would be impotent. Still, I think we can identify untoward forms of anger, just as we can distinguish healthy hunger from gluttony. Let me catalog some of the ways anger can go wrong.

First, it can be misdirected. Psychologists warn against the "fundamental attribution error," blaming an individual for actions that may owe more to circumstance. This happens when we blame drug and property crimes entirely on individuals, for example, without also seeing structural causes that may be somewhat exonerating.

Second, anger can be misattributed. Some people turn their self-dissatisfaction outward, and others bring workplace frustrations home, lashing out at the near and dear.

Third, anger can also spread too widely, as in Callard's example of harboring a grudge against all Germans; this may be instrumental when national values remain corrupt, but at a certain point, it becomes vital to distinguish those who work to combat bigotry and those who wax nostalgic for armbands and brownshirts.

Fourth, anger can be abusive. Consider the spouse who overreacts to minor mishaps with unpredictable fits of rage, or the tyrant who violently silences dissent. Anger is an instrument of both liberation and oppression.

Fifth, anger can reflect an undue sense of entitlement. Some people think they deserve special treatment and get bent out of shape when their expectations are not met. It is often said that men are more anger-prone than women, and this is a double injustice, since warranted female ire is suppressed, while frivolous male tantrums are indulged.

Sixth, anger can be self-destructive. Those who stew in rage may feel consumed by it. This does not mean that we should simply acquiesce to bad circumstances. But anger needs to find constructive outlets; the flames of rage scorch the torch when they cannot be used to ward off what ails us.

Seventh, just as pent-up rage is deleterious, harm can come from unleashing anger without restraint. It can trigger cycles of revenge. If restraint is exercised, the angry party can claim the moral high ground ("I gave you less than you deserved"), and that may reduce the likelihood of retaliation.

Such restraint brings us to a final issue: control. In moments of fury, we are not the best deliberators, and that fact, ironically, is an impediment to doing what anger demands of us.

In these and other ways, we can distinguish forms of anger that are better and worse. Callard might counter that the better forms still qualify as ordinary anger, albeit properly directed and proportionately applied. She wants mainly to reject those who posit a pristine species of anger, honorifically named "indignation," that is purged of its usual pugnaciousness. But to insist that anger has one form is overly reductive. Emotions are not mere instincts, hardwired in unchanging forms into our reptilian brains. They can also be retuned by cultural learning. In Malay, there are different words for brooding anger (*marah*) and frenzied rage (*amuk*). In the past, anger was more linked to violence than it is today, and that violence took culturally specific forms (such as dueling). These days anger might instead motivate legal action or "calling someone out" on social media.

In the end, then, Callard is right that we need anger, but we should not conceive of it as an untamable beast within. We can find forms that are most conducive to its varied vocations. Anger has a history, and it also has a future, which we can play an active role in shaping.

ACCOUNTABILITY WITHOUT VENGEANCE
Rachel Achs

AGNES CALLARD IS RIGHT that a retaliatory instinct is often rationally bound up with the way we hold each other morally accountable. But before we join her in bemoaning the impossibility of retaining innocence as a victim of injustice, it is worth scrutinizing the rationale that ties moral responsibility and retribution together. According to the "Argument for Revenge," retaliating against wrongdoers is a way of "teaching someone a lesson." But is it always the *only* way, or the best?

It seems to me that it depends—on what lesson we wish to teach, what the transgressor already knows, and what sort of admonishment might succeed in getting *this particular individual* to learn from my reciprocal anger.

Consider some examples. One lesson we might wish to impart on a wrongdoer is not to harm again in the same way. If you steal from me on Monday, I might hope to teach you not to do so again on Tuesday, nor, indeed, to steal from me ever again. Alternatively or additionally, we might hope that the offender comes to understand the wrongness of what she has done: to learn either *that* her behavior was wrong, *what it means* for her behavior to have been wrong, *which aspects* of her behavior made it wrong, and so on. I might wish for you to know, for example, that it is considered disrespectful to flout property rights, or to learn some of the ways that your theft inconvenienced me.

Yet it is far from clear that the best way to teach *all* these lessons, in *every* case, is by retaliating against the transgressor. Surely there are instances when alternative methods would be superior? For instance, perhaps in some scenarios a simple request would suffice to prevent the harm from being repeated—and have the added benefit of being much less likely to backfire. Nor will causing a wrongdoer to suffer help her to understand the wrongness of what she has done more deeply in those cases where she *already* possesses this sort of understanding.

One might defend retaliation against these charges by saying it is essential to convey to a wrongdoer how it felt to be a victim of what she did. Vengeance, on this line of thought, is always required to teach her *that*.

But this is either a lesson that can't be taught, or one for which retribution is likewise often unnecessary. If what we wish is for a wrongdoer to know *exactly how it felt* to experience what she did to us, then we are probably setting ourselves up for disappointment. After all, even retaliating against you with an eye for an eye won't make you feel what it was like to have the experience of being wronged *as me*. If, on the other hand, what we hope for is not complete immersion into our own psyches, but rather just that the people who wrong us come to develop some empathy with us as victims, then, again, retribution may sometimes be a useful tool, but it certainly won't always be a necessary one. In many cases the people who hurt us are people who have been hurt in the past themselves, and they are fully capable of putting themselves in our shoes by reflecting on their own past experiences. Retaliating *may* prompt this sort of reflection, but it may also just as well incite defensiveness.

I don't deny, then, that moral education might *sometimes* best be served by unleashing retaliatory anger on a wrongdoer. But it seems undeniable that there are plenty of instances in which alternative strategies would serve equally well, if not better, to achieve this end.

This analysis makes trouble for Callard's larger conclusion. If vengeance is really only fruitful in a subset of cases, it seems wrong to conclude that there is reason for revenge to be *the* way that humans hold one another responsible. At most, it looks like we can say that there is reason for revenge to be *a* way that *some* people can *sometimes* hold others responsible. This could hardly be described as a situation in which it is impossible for victims of injustice to avoid getting their hands dirty.

THERE IS A WAY out of this problem, though, because there is a different way to argue that retaliation is the right response to being wronged. Rather than contending that there is something *intrinsic* to vengeance that makes it especially edifying in any and all cases, we might instead begin with the observation that many humans, as a matter of convention, take revenge to be an appropriate response to wrongdoing. The reason for retaliation would then be the same one that people usually have to enact conventional norms: that conventions have communicative power. Just as one might communicate respect by adhering to certain norms of etiquette, or communicate one's thoughts by using linguistic conventions, so too does retaliating against those who have offended us communicate something—in this case, that we recognize we have been wronged.

If this is right, then anyone who is wronged does have *some* reason to retaliate. Avenging oneself is how a person can communicate that she perceives what has been done to her is a *wrongdoing*. Note that the communicative and educational justifications for vengeance are not necessarily incompatible. Insofar as it is important that this perception of wrongdoing be communicated to the perpetrator, we might still see the justification for vengeance as rooted in the value of educating wrongdoers. But whether or not the wrongdoer really listens to me in a particular instance, or really learns her lesson, may be of minimal importance. Instead, it might matter more to us to convey our perception of how we have been treated to other members of our community, or even just to mark it for ourselves.

Where does this leave us, then, with the question of innocence in the face of injustice? Is it possible, after all, to practice moral accountability without vengeance?

On the one hand, if the norm for responding to wrongdoing *is* to retaliate, then responding to an objectionable event in some other way isn't going to as successfully register that event as a wrong. For example, I take it that a powerful reason for discontent with German denazification after World War II was precisely that the absence or lightness of sentencing in many cases was inadequate to communicate the horrific nature of Nazi crimes. (This sort of pressure toward conservatism—reasons not to depart from or try to reform what we already do—arises in any norm-governed communicative context. Deviating from a convention, the worry goes, will fail to have the same communicative effect.)

On the other hand, it would seem that we have reason to be more optimistic than Callard is about the prospects of accountability becoming less vengeful. If the main justification for holding people responsible via retribution resides in the communicative power of conventions, then we can expect there to be plenty of instances in which the benefits of developing more humane ways of holding people responsible outweigh whatever value there is in retribution. A conservative might still worry, and rightly so, that violating the convention to retaliate may introduce communicative confusion: if we muddy the semiotic waters by transgressing communicative norms, we may fail to signal what we intend to get across. But absolute clarity doesn't always have to be our *top* priority—precisely because the limitations on what we can convey using reformed practices need only be temporary, since the fact that retribution holds so much communicative power stems merely from convention. Once new communicative conventions catch on, they may work just as well, or even better than, the old ones.

The upshot is that, while there is some reason that the affective response to injustice clings to the taste of blood, it doesn't have to cling quite so tightly.

WHAT'S PAST IS PROLOGUE
Barbara Herman

I CAN SEE THE POINT in Agnes Callard's observation that being the victim of wrongdoing is often worse for us than the harm done. The question is, even so, why not get over it? Callard thinks that even though the wrong recedes into the past, and even if there has been a sincere effort to make amends, we still have reason to be angry and to want revenge (whether or not we act on that desire). But why should the wrong in the past be eternally present *and* potent?

Many things happen that affect us and cause strong emotions. I discover wood rot in the window of my house and I am upset, even angry. I arrange to get the window fixed, and the feelings recede. A better paint job can make me think it was all to the good. It would make no sense to find that past event eternally upsetting even though, in a sense, the wood rot, as past, is eternally present. Why does Callard think the example of theft is different? The eternal reason for anger can't just be about the eternal present of the past. It must be that *a wrong* was done and apology is inefficacious in mitigating that.

Why might that be? Perhaps it is that the wrong done casts us as a victim. We can passively acquiesce to the bad treatment or wait for the wrongdoer to alter our narrative through apology and redress. Anger, by contrast, reclaims our agency—though at a price. It is a dark thing; surely unwelcome. Recasting it as indignation or righteous resistance doesn't change that. Whether we act on anger or not, it alters us, makes us worse—not who we would have been except for the wrongdoer's insult.

Suppose we agree that the issue is about regaining agency. Accepting an apology, though perhaps morally called for, doesn't put me back in my life's driver seat. Still, there are options. We could regard the apology as a first step and not a last one: an acknowledgment by the wrongdoer that how the future goes for us is now up to me. Things have to change, I say. There is work to be done. If we do the work, the wrong done remains where it was, but its teeth have been pulled. There's something to remember (and maybe never forget), but its narrative place in our lives has altered. The past that's in the present is different.

It is possible that whatever happened cannot be absorbed between us going forward. Perhaps it was too awful. But it isn't awfulness that Callard is pointing to: it's just the eternal past wrong in the present. Would Callard embrace the same logic for shame? Am I eternally bound to my own errors? (It is true that I can still activate the distress I felt when I was accused of and embarrassed by a clumsy act at age six, even though I know now that it was something we got over. It seems bizarre to me, not at all appropriate, maybe something to bring to my therapist, that I remain vulnerable to the memory of that past event.)

There is also a point in moral metaphysics here. Callard seems to think moral causality simply tracks natural causality. The moral event just is the natural event. But is that so? If we ask "When does an action or event end?" or "Which effects of an action belong to it?" the two causal orders can give different answers. My agential causality is morally salient even if absent my action the same effect would have occurred by other causes. I think that one of the tasks of morality—its duties, obligations, and responsive practices—is to supply a proprietary overlay on natural causality. There's reason to think that moral requirement functions as a kind of safe harbor. The untoward effects of morally required actions are not imputable to agents (given due care), whereas untoward effects of wrongful actions are imputable (because the agent on her own authority, not morality, has determined what is to be done).

Once we recognize the possible independence of moral from natural causality, backward moral effects are possible (it's no harder than coming to see a past event as a first step in an ongoing process). Moral causality can't change the material event—the thing was stolen on Monday—but we have public vehicles of redress that can negate the change in possession, mark the absence of permission, and block the perpetrator's authority over my narrative. I am not any longer a victim. It is now up to me whether to count your apology as a step forward. In standing with others, I have been given new powers.

So why might I still be angry? Set aside grown-up anger—indignation and the rest—and go back to where anger first appears. It is hard to imagine anyone angrier than a frustrated infant. Hungry; wet; hurting. Abandoned and alone. Panicked. Then saved: cosseted and returned to peace and love. The child learns to trust, but the body memory that the world can be lost remains. And so the anger. In the Monday theft, the moral injury is a reminder. I am (again) not self-sufficient. I am (again) vulnerable—always and fundamentally. The old anger returns. Infant anger is not directed at an episode: it is the infant in the moment. Regressive anger repeats the experience; it is timeless, a failure of the world. Reason to panic. The infant bites; it isn't punishment or revenge; she would consume the errant (m)other to become whole once again. This doesn't set a template for reasonable anger.

Is this a less plausible just-so story than Callard's? I can't see why it would be.

And what of Nietzschean ressentiment? Is it supporting evidence for Callard's idea of an anger-and-revenge-centric morality. What Nietzsche uncovers is the fear of the oppressed victim turned outward and into anger by priests who gain power by inverting the natural order of things, calling it morality. The believers learn to be oppressors too—of themselves. They could stay in this posture, waiting for someone or something to redeem them. We needn't dispute this history. Must it be true of us? We could instead together enact a less reactive moral order, one in which we add to our powers a "normative skin" that registers and sublimates the old anger, offering in its bloody stead a place in a social world that preserves dignity. We are injured; *we* pick us up; it is our story now; no reason to panic.

At the end, Callard wants us to see that "we can't be good in a bad world"—that it is impossible to respond rightly to being treated wrongly because, if we were honest, we'd admit that we want blood.

We want to turn the principle of wrongful action that victimized us on our victimizer. And two wrongs don't make a right.

There is truth in the observation that a bad world can make good action feel out of reach. What are we to do when kindness becomes an exploitable vulnerability or when our trust is consistently betrayed? In a bad world we feel passive, powerless, victims. Who wouldn't be angry? On Callard's picture, in teaching me eternal anger, the bad world owns me. It forever gives me reason to respond in kind. But why accept that? Surely *we* can build something that gets us past the eternal return of anger. My reason not to trust a past wrongdoer is not a reason to give up on trust.

Morality may have a dark history in primal anger and guilt that is hard to shed. But it is possible that the role of the dark side is to make vivid our wholeness in attachment to others, to give us confidence that a wrong done to us is not the end of the world. We are not alone. This is a hopeful view, not a timid one.

AGAINST MORAL PURITY

Oded Na'aman

START AT THE END: "We can't be good in a bad world." Agnes Callard's main claim is that the right moral response to injustice is a kind of anger that involves committing wrongs, sometimes very serious wrongs. Only in a world very different from our own, where people don't do bad things, could we avoid such "moral corruption." This conclusion is particularly surprising because, while taking herself to be arguing *against* a purified notion of morality, Callard seems to posit a moral standard none of us can hope to meet. How did Callard end up doubling down on moral purity?

To answer this question, we need to go back and follow the argument. Callard starts off by arguing that an apparent philosophical controversy about anger conceals a shared fantasy. Some philosophers believe the world would be better without anger, while others believe a certain form of anger is part of an appropriate moral response to wrongdoing. In fact, Callard argues, both camps reject two crucial characteristics of anger, namely, the tendency to bear a grudge despite the wrongdoer's attempts at restitution and the tendency to exact revenge. Philosophers have been striving to purify anger from these nasty tendencies by describing them as pathological and unreasonable. But Callard insists these philosophers' aim is unrealistic and their verdict is oblivious to the valid reasoning that supports the grudge-bearing and vengeful tendencies of anger.

Callard therefore offers arguments to the conclusion that bearing grudges and exacting revenge are rational and justified. First, she argues that since the wrong that is the reason for anger cannot be undone no matter what compensation is offered or how profusely and sincerely the wrongdoer apologizes, the reason for anger will remain. This conclusion justifies clinging to one's anger despite attempts at restitution. Second, Callard argues that revenge is how we hold each other responsible for wrongdoing: the wrong done to us is made into a general principle that is imposed on the wrongdoer. We teach the wrongdoer a lesson, she says, by making his bad our good. The first argument suggests that the moral sensibility of anger is a grudge-bearing sensibility, and the second suggests that anger is a mechanism for moral accountability through vengeance. We cannot cleanse anger from these tendencies without eliminating its primary moral functions.

Callard does not take the two arguments to be decisive, but she maintains they are simple, intuitive, and compelling. How could so many good philosophers fail to recognize them? The reason these arguments have been overlooked, Callard says, is that "we do not want to acknowledge the possibility that morally righteous anger provides rational grounds for limitless violence."

Na'aman

I think Callard is right that we resist the idea that limitless violence is rational and moral, but I also think we have good reason to resist it: it is outrageous. Given the implausibility of the conclusion, the arguments that lead to it better be decisive or else we should doubt the arguments' validity (that the conclusions follow from the premises) or soundness (that the premises are true). I will come back to this point because I believe Callard's argument for bearing grudges is not valid and her argument for revenge is not sound. But before I say more about these arguments, I want to continue tracing Callard's line of thought in order to explain how she ends up with a morally purified view of morality.

Callard says the arguments she presents lead to the conclusion that "the morally correct way to respond to immorality is to do things—cling to anger, exact vengeance—that are in some way immoral." What does Callard mean by this? If grudge-bearing, vengeful anger is a morally appropriate response, then in what sense is it immoral? And if anger is immoral then in what sense is it morally righteous? Callard has an answer: "just because the moral corruption of anger is our best option doesn't mean it is not corruption." Given the fact of wrongdoing, some amount of grudge-bearing, vengeful anger is our best moral option. But our best moral option still involves moral corruption ("violence," "bloodlust"), so moral goodness in response to wrongdoing is impossible for us and, consequently, we can't be morally good in this bad world.

I believe this purified view of morality is misguided. Saying that a good person must be a person who never encounters moral wrongdoing is like saying that a healthy person must be a person who never falls ill. Such a healthy, good person could not live among us humans. We—human beings—develop physical and moral resilience by encountering disease and wrongdoing, not by avoiding them. For us, being healthy involves managing our physical vulnerability well and being good involves managing our moral vulnerability well. And, just as a healthy response to sickness can defeat the disease without amplifying or spreading it, a moral response to wrongdoing can address the wrong without replicating it. Human health is conditioned on the inevitability of disease; human goodness is conditioned on the inevitability of wrongdoing.

To be sure, Callard is right that grudge-bearing, vengeful anger is morally corrupt, but I believe she is wrong that it is a morally correct response to wrongdoing. In fact, we are often very angry indeed (and for good reason) without being inclined to bear grudges or exact revenge. Consider again the argument for bearing grudges. The wrong that is the reason for anger will never be undone, Callard says, so the reason for anger remains forever. But the wrong and its status as a reason for anger are two different things. While the wrong will remain, it might cease to *be* a reason for anger. The significance of past events can change in light of subsequent occurrences: my friend has apologized for betraying my trust, she sincerely regrets it, and we talked it over, so her betrayal might no longer be a reason for anger on my part. The betrayal remains the same, and just as wrong as it was, but its moral significance changes in light of the way it was addressed. So, from the fact that the wrong remains forever, it doesn't follow that the reason for anger remains forever. The argument for bearing grudges is not valid.

Na'aman

Now consider the argument for revenge. Callard says that revenge is how we hold each other accountable, so it is essential to the accountability mechanism of anger. But even if revenge is *a* way to hold a person accountable, it does not seem to be the only way. Though Callard focuses on egregious wrongs, most of the mundane wrongs we encounter in the course of our daily lives do not prompt us to seek revenge. In fact, almost every meaningful relationship involves some instances of wrongdoing, which may even strengthen the relationship if they lead to a clarification of its essential norms, expectations, and boundaries. When I feel wronged by a family member, friend, or lover, I am not inclined "to make her bad my good," but I certainly want to hold her accountable, and I seek her recognition of the wrong she has done to me. Since revenge is not necessary for accountability, the argument for revenge is not sound.

Though we are not forced to accept Callard's "devastating conclusion"—that limitless violence is morally and rationally justified—Callard calls our attention to a deep and important fact: an appropriate response to wrongdoing may sometimes involve the intentional infliction of suffering on others. This should not lead us to lament the existence of wrongdoing in our world, but to recognize that suffering has a place in our moral ideals. You can't be good without experiencing some bad.

THE WOUND IS REAL

Agnes Callard

PAUL BLOOM ASKS, "Do angry people make the best romantic partners?" "Best" is a tricky word here, but speaking only for myself, I
would not think that the "best" partner for me would be someone
who never became angry or even someone who became angry less
frequently than my husband does.

I am not perfect. Sometimes I am insufficiently loving, apprecia-
tive, or attentive; sometimes I do not try hard enough to overcome my
faults; and sometimes I behave in ways that are outright disrespectful.
Because he loves me, my husband doesn't just observe or notice my
disrespect, he directly undergoes or experiences it. My disrespect
hits him where it hurts, and his anger hits back, and hurts me. If he
became less sensitized to how I act, or if I became less sensitive to
his anger, I would not see that as an improvement in our relationship.
Rather, I would think that we had come to matter less to one another.

One reason why we want romantic partners in the first place is
that we need help to become the people we want to be—we are not,

already, "best." When you have a deep connection with someone, their anger allows you to outsource some of your striving: your partner's anger is a mechanism of your aspiration. Daryl Cameron and Victoria Spring are right to note that making use of this mechanism has real psychological costs. Nonetheless, I want my husband to be willing to shoulder such costs on my behalf. I see his willingness to devote some of himself to regulating me—to dedicate a piece of his own psychological real estate to combating my faults and vices—as a measure of his love.

Of course this system can go haywire, as in cases of abuse. And, if activated too often, it is liable to generate a deadening hardness: the barrier between a high-conflict couple can become so thick that it can be pierced only by escalating to an extreme level of nastiness. But those are the failure cases, and they shouldn't distract us from the existence of success cases. In fact, as Jesse Prinz emphasizes, the very fact that there are characteristic ways for anger to go wrong suggests that there is something to the idea that it can go right.

So, I disagree with Bloom's conception of anger as a sickness, best eradicated, or—if that should prove impossible—lessened. Instead I join Oded Na'aman in thinking that anger is part of a healthy human life, though I also continue to maintain that there is something unhealthy about even the healthiest—that is, most successful—cases of anger.

As an analogy, consider a fever. When you are feverish, you are not healthy, in that you cannot engage in your normal, productive functions. Something is wrong with you; your body is awry; fever is a form of sickness. But a fever is also a healthy immune response to the presence in your body of some kind of infection. If I lost my susceptibility for fever, that would be a sign that things had gone *very* wrong—it would be a way of getting sicker, not healthier. So, while it is clearly not "best" to be weak, feverish, sleepy, and incapacitated, it might nonetheless be the best option on the table. A fever is a healthy way of being sick. I have much the same view about anger—although here "health" becomes a metaphor, and it is best to speak more directly of whether anger is rational, or the degree to which it is a genuine response to moral reasons.

Bloom questions whether the language of reasons is even appropriate in this context—do people get angry "for reasons" and can someone be "rationally" angry? I would note that we do tend to speak in both of these ways. In fact anger is one of the contexts where we take "reasons-speak" to be not only warranted but required. Consider some perfectly ordinary scenarios where this demand *isn't* made. We usually take ourselves to have reasons for what we are doing, but sometimes when someone asks me, "Why are you tapping your fingers like that?" or "Why did you suddenly start running?" I face no strenuous objection if all I have to offer by way of a response is, "No particular reason." Likewise, I sometimes know why I feel sad, but at other times I just feel sad "for no reason." In stark contrast, no one considers it acceptable to feel angry at a person for no reason. We may not be able (or wish) to articulate the reason, but we feel called upon—compelled—to try. When it comes to practical reasons—theoretical reasons, such as those involved in syllogistic argumentation, are a different matter—I can think of no attitude more implicated in the practice of giving and receiving them than anger. This is why Rachel Achs is absolutely right to emphasize the "communicative" function of anger.

As a counterpoint to Bloom, who thinks that I make anger sound too rational, consider Na'aman's argument that anger is in fact more rational—or at any rate less grudging and vengeful—than I claim it to be. I argued that if we have a reason to be angry, that reason never goes away or changes. Na'aman claims, to the contrary, that subsequent events can change the significance of a past action in such a way as to eliminate a reason for being angry. His examples of such significance-changers are apology and regret, which make it the case that my reason for being angry—your betrayal—"was addressed." But he does not say how apology and regret address someone's anger over a betrayal. One can, I admit, imagine a funny case in which my anger is not aroused by your betrayal of me—I'm fine with you betraying me!—but simply by the fact that that betrayal has gone unregretted and unapologized for. Once you regret and apologize, you have indeed "addressed" my grievance, and I no longer have any reason to be angry with you. But usually what I'm angry about is not the absence of measures to rectify a wrong but the presence of wrongdoing. And my claim was: because *that* doesn't change, *it* cannot be "addressed."

Barbara Herman argues along lines similar to Na'aman's when she proposes that there can be backward causation in the moral domain, and that this is "no more difficult to understand than coming to see a past event as a first step in an ongoing process." But consider an example of the latter: I see you laying bricks on the ground, thinking you are creating an artwork, and then later I realize you were laying the foundation of a house. I can say, "When I first assessed those bricks as an artwork, I was mistaken, because I didn't realize they were part of an ongoing process." The parallel is then: when I became angry at you for betraying me, I was mistaken, because I didn't realize that was part of an ongoing process that would end with you apologizing.

This doesn't seem right, and it suggests that backward moral causation is, indeed, much more difficult to understand than coming to see a past event as a first step in an ongoing process.

My point here is not quite the one Elizabeth Bruenig takes me to be making—that holding on to anger is in one's self-interest—but rather that holding on to anger is inscribed in the logic of anger. Bruenig herself gestures at this logic with her lovely description of anger's point of view as a "kingdom of damage." I am arguing that forgiveness has no location in that kingdom, even in cases where one might be selfishly benefitted by forgiving. It is not uncommon for someone to be unwilling to let go of anger even when the incentives for doing so are very great. She doesn't care about those rewards, or being happy, or the overall satisfaction of her preferences; she cares about one thing—the moral fact that, if I am right, continues to constitute a reason for her to be angry.

I do not deny that there might be some way to articulate what it might mean to change the (significance of the) moral facts, but I think that successfully doing so is much trickier than Herman or Na'aman present it to be. Those who would rescue forgiveness must face the eternal anger argument head on—and it is a formidable foe.

STILL, I admit that it is one thing to claim that the reasons for anger are eternal, and another to insist that they underwrite vengeance. Na'aman contends that I overstate the role of vengeance in anger, particularly in the case of those we are closest to. But I would note that we are reluctant to describe practices we ourselves are involved in as "vengeance." For instance, consider criminal justice. We do not feel that the wrongdoer has been held accountable unless he suffers for what he has done. We make his bad our good, and that is vengeance, even if we prefer to call it "retributive punishment." Likewise, I would call it "vengeance" when you are fighting with your spouse and deliberately say things you know will hurt them; or when you "punish" them by leaving dirty dishes for them to do; or demand that they perform whatever tasks—cleaning the living room, dealing with the car registration—you know they most hate. "Passive aggression" is one of the terms we use for small acts of vengeance that we prefer not to call "vengeance." I admit there is an approach to marital disputes that is entirely forward-looking, productive, and cheerful: "Can we do things differently in the future?" But note that such a Cheerfully Productive Spouse prescinds from the project of holding her spouse accountable—for that (backward-looking) project cannot, I maintain, be separated from wanting them to suffer in some way.

What is the force of acknowledging that our anger, even at its healthiest, is nonetheless still sick? If you can't be good in a bad world, then those whose anger is fully justified—the oppressed, the disenfranchised, and those who crusade angrily on their behalf—are tainted by moral imperfection. Desmond Jagmohan and Myisha Cherry are concerned that in pointing this out, my aim is to blame, judge, or censure such people, or to suggest that it would be "best"—to reprise Bloom's word—for them to be morally purer than they are.

In fact I agree with Cherry (herself echoing Amia Srinivasan) that "even if anger at racial injustice is counterproductive, it is still appropriate." And my emphasis on the connection between anger and holding accountable helps explain why this is true. As I see it, our concern with morality runs deeper than it being something we cheerfully hope to bring about: we are attached to it, and this attachment underwrites the importance of (backward-looking) considerations of accountability. Like Cherry, I believe this can be traced to the emotion of *love*.

One can't love a principle. When someone loves justice or equality, her love is, in the first instance, directed at the people—friends, associates, neighbors, fellow citizens, fellow humans—in whom those relations are, or should be, embodied. Love is a form of attachment, and therefore an avenue of vulnerability. Those who crusade for justice and equality by way of love open themselves up to being damaged and wounded in the face of injustice and inequality. Such people make a profound sacrifice, and we cannot be properly grateful to them for it without acknowledging that the wound—which takes the form of a fever of grudging vengeance—is real.

THE RADICAL EQUALITY OF LIVES
Judith Butler interviewed by Brandon M. Terry

JUDITH BUTLER IS arguably the most influential critical theorist of our era. Her early books, such as *Gender Trouble* (1990) and *Bodies That Matter* (1993), anticipated a profound social and intellectual upheaval around sex, sexuality, gender norms, and power. Like many readers of my generation, I was introduced to Butler's work just as these changes began to accelerate, and her ideas became part of mainstream discourse. In recent years, Butler has turned her insights about norms and exceptions, the psychic life of power, and the politics of resistance toward political ethics. In December Butler and I discussed her latest book, *The Force of Nonviolence*, which explores "nonviolence" as a project capable not simply of disclosing structural and repressive forms of violence, but also of productively channeling the tensions of social life away from retribution and resentment toward a radical and redemptive notion of equality.

—Brandon M. Terry

BRANDON TERRY: You begin *The Force of Nonviolence* with a problem that hangs heavily over contemporary debates within social movements and in some corners of academia: How does an apparently moral argument about whether to be for or against violence quickly turn into a debate about how violence is defined and who is called "violent"? For example, activists in the Movement for Black Lives have described a wide range of social phenomena, from mass incarceration to dominant norms around gender and sexuality, as state violence. Their critics meanwhile have accused them of promoting or inciting violence, especially against police officers. And as you point out, these attributions have real consequences, as we can see with DeRay McKesson, the Black Lives Matter leader being sued by a police officer injured at a protest McKesson organized.

Some worry that the idea of violence today has become an unsustainable inflation of the concept that renders it incapable of doing the normative or analytical work that some activists and scholars are asking it to perform. They worry that without a clear and constrained definition of violence, one on which we could get some consensus, our uses of the term are going to lead our moral judgment astray. It will make public debate even more acrimonious. You seem to be skeptical about these criticisms, and you even charge them with a bit of political and critical naivete. How do you see the link between the ethical critique of violence and the interrogation of how and why we name certain practices or phenomena violent?

JUDITH BUTLER: *The Force of Nonviolence* is not primarily about violence, it's about nonviolence, and whether it can still be defended, given all the realistic and strategic arguments against it. And yet, in order to make an argument for nonviolence, one needs to know what violence is; if the book's general claim is that we ought to be refraining from violence, we still need to be able to identify violence. That's where this complex question arises: How do we identify violence? What forms does violence take?

There's no easy answer to that question, but I would say that very often moral arguments about nonviolence tend to imagine an individual making a decision about whether or not to engage in an act of violence, either to hit someone, or to use an instrument to injure somebody, to use a gun or some military weapon, and yet violence cannot be restricted to the form of the single blow. We know that there are forms of violence that don't involve inflicting a blow on another person. The minute we accept that there is such a thing as institutional violence, or indeed symbolic violence, we are in a much more complex field. But I don't think we should throw up our hands and say, "Oh well this is all too fuzzy, we can't make our way here." Michel Foucault distinguished between forms of sovereign violence, whereby a king, a monarch, or someone vested with a sovereign power, decides who should live and who should die. And there's a form of violence that he called biopolitical and that Cameroonian philosopher Achille Mbembe calls necropolitics: violence that leaves a set of people to die, abandons them to death, or refuses to offer the assistance that is necessary in order to save their lives.

Those policies and institutions that let people die—that take away food stamps, or take away health care, or take away shelter—are not only exposing people to mortality, they're exposing people to mortality at differential rates. In the United States, we see that black and brown people, who are disproportionately poor in this country, are differentially exposed to that kind of violence and that kind of mortality rate. So maybe nobody is hitting them with a stick, or shooting them in the head, but there is an institutional violence at work, one which distinguishes between lives worth preserving and lives regarded as not worth preserving. So a differential calculus is at work, and it's an implicit feature of policies and institutions like that. That's one way of understanding institutional violence.

We could also look at the violence of carceral institutions in the ways that Ruth Gilmore, or Angela Davis, or Michelle Alexander have done. Violent criminals are sent to prison to punish their violence, and yet what they enter into is another form of violence, one that is understood as legally justified. It's not called violence, it's called "necessary coercion," or "necessary containment," or incarceration, but it is often a form of violence, especially in the way people are treated and how their lives are regarded, and the kind of violence to which they are subjected—daily, psychically—within the prison facility. So we can start to think about institutions as violent. But they're not just inflicting institutional violence. They are themselves violent institutions.

When we say we're opposed to violence, or we are seeking to embrace a philosophy and a politics of nonviolence, we are obligated to distinguish among those kinds of violence, to rely on our colleagues who have been doing important empirical and sociological work and cultural analysis to show us when and how violence happens and to whom—to whom does it happen more than others, and what radical thesis about the inequality of lives pervades these disparities.

BT: I am reminded of the essay you contributed to Robert Gooding-Williams's volume *Reading Rodney King* (1993), where you focus on racial fantasies, or "racial phantasms" as you call them, following Frantz Fanon. What do you think makes race-thinking so amenable to our judgments about who or what is violent?

JB: You're right. In this book I'm elaborating and revising the thesis I put forward in that essay. But in this context, I'm trying to understand why certain actions are called violent when there's no empirical, or visual, or testimonial evidence to corroborate that claim. As you know, the Rodney King beating was already pretty outrageous, although certainly not unusual for black people, who live in worlds where police violence is constant. King was on the ground. He was not sitting up, he was not standing up. He was barely moving a limb, and somehow that video could be pointed to in a trial, and the defense attorney for the police could claim that King was a threat. And it's really hard to understand how a black man lying on the ground, or indeed a black man running away, or a black man in a full chokehold, could still threaten the life of a policeman. And I think we could say that those are primarily states of the black body—social and political states of paralysis, threat, fear—none of which are arguably threatening, that are nevertheless cast, phantasmagorically, as states of imminent danger: as if those bodies are about to spring, to kill, to inflict mortal danger on the police who are, in fact, inflicting mortal danger.

We could point to that and just say, "Well, that's absurd," or we could say, "That's unjust," and we would be right. But we need to look a little bit more closely at what I call a "phantasmagoric inversion." It is not uncommon for the forces that inflict violence to point to their victims and say, "Look, this is the victim who's actually inflicting violence on me." And that's a trick of the mind, it's a trick of the culture, and it's a fantasy that gets shared when judges and juries look at the same evidence and decide that the policeman was just doing his job, or had good reason to think he was in trouble, or that a black man could have turned around and shot him at any moment. They are living in a panicked racial phantasm. They are in a war against black people in which they constantly imagine that those upon whom they inflict violence are the true source of violence.

BT: How do we find our way out? I'm thinking about a powerful point in the book where you contrast your approach with a methodological and ethical individualism. We're often given a genealogy of nonviolence that emphasizes individualism and a personal conscience, sometimes conscripting people such as Henry David Thoreau into this genealogy, and often treating nonviolence as kind of a retreat from the storm and stress of politics into a pacific region of the soul. In the book you say forcefully that this is a profound misdescription of the ethics and politics of nonviolence. You write, "an ethics of nonviolence cannot be predicated on individualism and must take the lead in critiquing individualism as the basis of ethics and politics."

Can you say more about what you see as the real connective tissue between this critique of individualism and nonviolence?

JB: If I am to understand myself as interconnected with other living beings and with life processes more generally, including all those that sustain the planet, I have to understand that when I destroy another person, or when I destroy a set of living processes, I also destroy something of myself, because the self that I am is not just this bounded and discrete ego, it's a set of relationships. I generally hold to the importance of psychosocial studies and believe my book probably belongs to that field. None of us exist or survive without a set of relationships that sustain us. That ideal might be maddening to a fierce individualist who wants to understand themself as completely self-sufficient, but the ideal of self-sufficiency is a bit destructive. We live in families and communities, and we're also, as we know from climate change, interconnected across the entire globe. We know forms of interdependency throughout the economic world through the ravaging effects of globalization. We need to come up with another notion of the global that would avow, affirm, and strengthen our interdependency, and also the fact that we're equally dependent on the Earth. We should strive to be equally dependent upon one another.

So for me, the idea of equality is not, "Oh, this individual's equal to another," although sometimes we must speak that way and have policies that reflect that truth. To shift the way we think about equality to help us address violence—and possibly also climate preservation—we need to move away from the ego and moral ideals of self-sufficiency. That is one reason I don't stress the virtue of equanimity that many classical philosophers in the West have approved. One finds it in Buddhism and other religions as well. I'm not opposed to equanimity—it's great to be calm and pacific and be able to handle life with some equanimity. I just don't believe it can be the basis of nonviolence. We have every reason to be absolutely enraged by the systemic and local injustices in our world. Not a day goes by under the present regime when I'm not seized with rage of one kind or another. The question is: What can be done with rage? We don't always think about that, because we view rage as an uncontrollable impulse that needs to come out in unmediated forms. But people craft rage, they cultivate rage, and not just as individuals. Communities craft their rage. Artists craft rage all the time. Collective forms of crafting rage are important. They don't deny rage, but they also choose not to enter into the cycle of violence. They seek to expose violence and counter it. We could have an angry and rageful art practice that exposes and counters violence without being violent. Being contaminated by violence is not the same as reproducing the systemic or institutional violence that we're seeking to oppose.

For me, the bottom line is that if I destroy another life, I also destroy myself to some degree, because relations compose who I am, and I am nothing without them. My life is not sustainable without others, and theirs is not sustainable without me. We're attacking the social bond that holds us together when we attack each other. And I believe we need to cultivate that kind of ethos in order to support a broader global philosophy and politics that is committed to radical equality and affirms the equal grievability of lives—the equal value of lives.

BT: Climate change seems to play for you the role that nuclear war played for a lot of the sixties theorists of nonviolence—the invention of nuclear weapons and the threat of extinction-level events forced them to think about interconnection, interdependency at the level of ontology, social ontology. Climate change has now superseded that in some ways and gives a kind of heft to the sort of thing you'd hear Martin Luther King, Jr., say often, about being in "an inescapable network of mutuality," or a "single garment of destiny."

But in response, as King's Black Power critics might say: "Well sure, people are interdependent, nobody is sufficient in and of themselves, we need communities to survive, we just don't want to be in a community with these people who have oppressed us any longer. We find living in social bonds with them to be something that is mutilating to our cultural vitality, and our self-respect." What do you think is wrong with the longing to reconstitute mutuality in more restricted terms in pursuit of these goods?

JB: All relations among humans are vexed, and difficult, and even relations of love are structured by ambivalence. They carry within them destructive potential, and those of us who work to acknowledge the destructive potential in our relationships are better equipped to avoid acting destructively than those who pretend that there is no destructive potential. One reason I don't hold to the notion that we need to reside in the pacific rooms of the soul at the expense of other or different rooms is that we need to struggle with our anger, our destructiveness, even our murderous impulse. We need to accept that we have all of that. Now I think among people who agree to cohabit

Earth—as Hannah Arendt put it in her theorizations, among other places, about the state of Israel in relationship to the emergent state of Palestine—there does not have to be love or harmony or even high levels of integration for there to be a basic respect for the lives of others and as a premise for any kind of collaboration or integration, an acceptance of the radical equality of lives. Without those, any other form of social belonging or cohabitation reproduces inequality. And who wants that? People don't want to live with others who despise them, or mutilate them, or regard their lives as dispensable, or who are willing to adopt and implement policies that have that effect. So there has to be a radical agreement to this equality for a kind of cohabitation to take place that would be worthy of the name.

BT: Let's explore this question of equality. As somebody who's followed your work for a long time, I think that the book develops some long-standing themes: your interrogation of the fraught relationship of norm and exception in politics, and your linkage—especially in your work on Antigone and the series of books beginning with *Frames of War* (2009)—between questions of equality and questions of grief and mourning. You've done a lot to show us how certain populations and groups are figured as beyond the reach of humane concern and solidarity by interrogating practices of mourning and grieving as points of access, places where we might know what and whom we value, whom we imagine our lives entangle with and are enriched by, and even who counts as human. In *The Force of Nonviolence* you talk not just about equality but what you call "the radical equality of grievability." That is such a poignant phrase. What might such an ideal entail in practice, and why connect it to the politics of nonviolence, instead of just making it, say, a principle of justice?

JB: Some people don't like this word, "grievable." It's an awkward word. "Grievability" may be even worse, but I'm trying to get at a quality of life. We say certain deaths aren't grievable, or haven't been properly grieved. We talk that way all the time. But I'm referring to people who are living in this world, and who feel themselves to be living a life that will not be mourned when it is lost, or who look at others and regard them as lives that will not be mourned if they are lost.

When we talk that way about ourselves or others, what we're really saying is that while these are lives that can pass without a trace—one could think, for example, of those who fell or were thrown into the ocean during the Middle Passage—how do we mourn them, and what does it mean that those lives were considered ungrievable? There would be no one to grieve them, there's nothing in them to be grieved. There's not value to be grieved. And I think that's another way of getting to what some would call dehumanization, a term that we could talk about, but I'm not sure it grasps everything.

Grievability is a way of thinking about value. I remember Claudia Rankine published an article in the *New York Times* in 2015 called "'The Condition of Black Life Is One of Mourning.'" She talks about the sense of anxiety and fear that mothers have—though not just mothers—that bringing African American men and women into the world is bringing them into a place of potential mourning. They may be lost. They may be extinguished. They may not survive. And she writes about what it means to have a sense that lives may be lost at any moment, or that the world does not have to seek to sustain those lives and does not recognize the value of those lives. Of course, this is not a totalizing claim, but this risk is higher for some than for others.

Equal grievability would mean that each life has a value and is regarded as a life worthy of living, to be lived, deserving to be lived. There can be no inequality there. Now, that's an ideal, a norm, a principle, and that's what I mean by the notion of radical equality. If we had it and we had our understanding of ourselves as socially interdependent creatures, we would have a broader understanding of what it means to oppose violence. And I'm not interested in establishing nonviolence as an absolute moral principle that has to be applied to every instance. I'm interested in cultivating a new sense of who we are as human beings and how we treat each other on the basis of an interdependent ontology, if you will, with a historical, political mindfulness about the unequal grievability of lives in our contemporary world. Justice is great, but it would be more probable in a world in which we'd learned to think clearly about who suffers violence disproportionately and who inflicts it disproportionately.

BT: What's always drawn me to this line of inquiry is that it makes so much sense of a lot of African American protest and African American mourning practices. The civil rights movement is shot through with all of these concerns. Why didn't President Lyndon Johnson meet with the parents of slain African American activist James Chaney, but *did* meet with the parents of Chaney's slain white colleagues, Andrew Goodman and Michael Schwerner? Why were Memphis sanitation workers Echol Cole and Robert Walker allowed to die in the back of a garbage truck, launching that protest movement that would ultimately bring King to the place where he would be assassinated? Even W. E. B. Du Bois's *The Souls of Black Folk* (1903) dwells on this question, from his mentor to his own dying infant son: If you're born in a society like this, will your life be grievable? Will anyone mourn your passing? Will you have any potential or possibility or standing as a cocreator of the society? Or are you already diminished?

JB: The question is also linked with whether your life will be liveable? Will you survive, will you persist, and will the conditions of life allow you to flourish? Some populations dispossess those who are subject to racism, to economic marginalization, or genocidal violence. They live with that question or have given up on that question.

BT: What is so striking about the language of equal grievability is that it also makes sense of King's intervention. He said many of the same things you're saying, but in his embodied performance, he also tried to disrupt that systemic violence without inviting the destruction of the lives of either the authors or ignoble spectators of oppression. He wanted to preserve his *enemies'* lives as well.

To me that it the most dramatic demonstration of somebody who really believes in the equal grievability of lives. Should we read you as endorsing, or at least having a family resemblance with, King's judgment that it is better to take on more suffering than you dispense?

JB: I don't know, but I do think that there are a lot of people who have every reason to feel enormous rage, to imagine scenes of destruction, and to even be overwhelmed with murderous feelings or impulsse. The question is: To what community do we turn in such moments so that we don't reproduce and heighten a violent world? I think of the idea of preserving the life of the one you want to kill as preserving the world you want to fight for, the world in which this kind of violence is lessened rather than heightened. And so it's for the world, for a very difficult social bond, one that is full of passion, ecstatic and wonderful, but is also destructive and horrid. I guess I'm willing to take that point from Sigmund Freud; I think Fanon got it. Our relationships with others have this vexed quality. They can lift us and they can debase us, and we have to find our way. I think that those have to be collective practices; I'm not as interested in acts of individual heroism. I worry sometimes that the civil rights movement, or at least the *story* that gets told about it in the United States, focuses on individual heroes and heroines.

I don't want it to be a model of an individual, I want it to be a different kind of sociality that we're trying to build, and I do see it in some of the social movements today, in some of the ways that people are working on housing projects, and climate preservation, and climate activism. I see it in many different parts of the world. In the feminist movement, in the Black Lives Matter movement. It's not always easy. We struggle, we fight, we disagree, but we come back somehow to continue to build a world that is less violent and more free and more equal. And I think if we want to talk about justice, it would have to have all those components.

BT: You end the book with reference to some of these movements —Ni Una Menos, the protests at the European refugee camps, the Standing Man protest in Turkey. I, like you, take a lot of hope from these practices. But as a scholar of black protest movements, I wonder if maybe the long-term threat to nonviolent action is not that it would be falsely characterized as violent, but that it gets absorbed into our sense of the everyday and becomes what King called "a merely transitory drama." That it becomes ritualized or folded into our sense of, "That's what these kinds of people do." What if it becomes a spectacle that fails to unsettle or even register as spectacle, and that might be in part because it's *not* considered violence or violent enough. What do you think might break through our existing attention economy and media environment that are arguably fascinated with violence above all else?

JB: You're right to name the media, because I think more and more what we see happening, especially with violence in schools, is that kids, you know, even when they commit suicide, say, "Well, this was the only way to get my name in the newspaper, this was my only way to get attention." What are they responding to? They're on social media, they're on the internet, and they see that an act of violence appears to break through quotidian life and grab worldwide attention. Now, the problem with that media rhythm—and there is a pattern that social media and conventional media have developed—is that it suggests that quotidian life is not violent, even though there are huge amounts of domestic violence, violence in prison, violence on the street, and violence in the workplace all the time. Actual quotidian violence gets repainted as nonviolent, and then the very dramatic violence catches attention, but only for a moment because the next one is on its way, and the next one is in competition with the last one.

We need to think more clearly about a media presence that counters that particular rhythm, which propagates a certain kind of lie about what violence is. It becomes a sensationalist moment, rather than part of the structure of life. We need to turn a lens on the forms of violence that are part of the structure of life for women, for minorities, for the dispossessed, for the poor. Until we do that, we will continue to think that violence is this extraordinary thing that captures attention for a minute and is then dispensed with. So we have a broader problem in thinking about how the media covers violence, and how it tends to define it, which means that cultural workers and academics and artists who are really concerned with this issue need to develop a stronger media presence, or maybe even a counter-media presence, to shift the terms.

BT: A profoundly difficult challenge, indeed, but with the proliferation of cameras, the low barrier of entry to social media distribution, and the increasingly sophisticated popular criticism of media frames and narrative strategies, perhaps we might yet see our way out. Another set of crucial questions, from an exciting book full of them.

JB: That's very kind, thank you so much.

A HISTORY OF ANGER
David Konstan

ANGER, LIKE OTHER EMOTIONS, has a history.

It is not merely that the causes of anger may change, or attitudes toward its expression. The nature of the emotion itself may alter from one society to another. In classical antiquity, for example, anger was variously viewed as proper to a free citizen (an incapacity to feel anger was regarded as slavish); as an irrational, savage passion that should be extirpated entirely, and especially dangerous when joined to power; as justifiable in a ruler, on the model of God's righteous anger in the Bible; and as blasphemously ascribed to God, who is beyond all human emotions.

Profound social and cultural changes—the transition from small city-states to the vast reach of the Roman Empire, the adoption of Christianity as the official religion of Rome—lay behind these shifting views, but all the positions had their defenders and were fiercely debated. This rich heritage offers a wealth of insights into the nature of anger, as well as evidence of its social nature; it is not just a matter of biology. Anger's history—along with the very fact that it has one—can shed light on the hypertrophied emotional climate of today.

ANGER WAS PRESENT at the very beginning of classical civilization, pervading its two foundational epics, Homer's *Iliad* and *Odyssey*. Indeed, the first word of the Iliad is *mênis*, an elevated term bearing something of the tone of "wrath." It refers to Achilles's rage, which will break out after he is insulted by Agamemnon, and which will dominate the poem until the end, when Achilles kills Hector in order to avenge the death of his dearest friend, Patroclus. The *Odyssey*, in turn, is the story of a hero who returns home after the Trojan War, only to find 108 young men in his house, all suing for the hand of his wife and vying to take his role as prince of Ithaca. Odysseus does not stop fighting until every last one of them is dead.

The Homeric epics revolve around a kind of warrior code in which fury is glorified. But as historian William Harris suggests in his book *Restraining Rage* (2004), the following centuries saw a kind of civilizing process at work: civic society developed a sense that anger must be moderated. Writing roughly 400 years after Homer, for example, Aristotle warned that irascibility—too quick a temper—indicated a lack of moral self-control. The fact that anger could easily get out of control and produce real harm led him to regard it as especially dangerous—in contrast, say, to emotions such as pity or shame.

Moreover, anger, in Aristotle's view, is not simply a feeling or a reaction, devoid of reason; instead, it *responds* to reasons and involves cognition. "Let anger be a desire," he wrote in *Rhetoric*, "accompanied by pain, for a perceived revenge, on account of a perceived slight on the part of people who are not fit to slight one or one's own." For Aristotle, the primary stimulus to anger is the judgment or perception that we have been slighted or put down. It follows, he says, that we cannot be angry at an inanimate thing or an animal—since they may hurt us but do not insult us—and also that anger is associated with status.

Indeed, Aristotle's view of anger is well suited to the competitive world of the classical democratic city-state, where citizens were alert to protecting their dignity in the face of both the rich and powerful and the more humble, who might challenge the implicit social hierarchy. Hence the provision that anger responds to a slight on the part of those who are not fit to insult you. An affront on the part of a superior is not the same as one delivered by an inferior. Slaves, he says, are expected to swallow any resentment they might feel toward their masters; indeed, he suggests that the powerless are incapable of feeling anger at all: "No one gets angry at someone when it is impossible to achieve revenge, and with those who are far superior in power than themselves people get angry either not at all or less so." On the other hand, a free person would never be expected to endure a comparable insult without irritation. As he says in the *Nicomachean Ethics*, that would constitute a sign of servility, not of tolerance or noble temperament.

YET ANGER LOOKS VERY DIFFERENT from the perspective of its victims, and the philosophical tradition of Stoicism, which originated in the increasingly autocratic world after Aristotle's death, entertained a suspicion of all emotions, above all anger. Writing roughly 300 years after Aristotle, the philosopher Seneca produced the most detailed treatise on anger that has come down from antiquity. He offers a variety of shocking illustrations of how the anger of people with absolute power could have appalling consequences (as the anger of masters did in respect to slaves throughout classical antiquity). Describing the Roman statesman Gnaeus Piso, for example, Seneca says he was "a man free from many vices, but misguided, in that he mistook inflexibility for firmness." Piso ordered the execution of one of his soldiers when the soldier returned without his comrade, reasoning that the soldier must have killed him. But just as the soldier was presenting his neck to the executioner, the missing man appeared, and the executioner spared him. The crowd rejoiced, but "Piso mounted the tribunal in a rage," Seneca writes:

> and ordered both soldiers to be led to execution, the one who had done no murder and the one who had escaped it. . . . And Piso added a third. He ordered the centurion who had brought back the condemned man to be executed as well. On account of the innocence of one man, three were appointed to die in the self-same place. How clever is anger in devising excuses for its madness. . . . It thought out three charges because it had grounds for none.

Konstan

From today's vantage point, such a violent disposition is regarded as wholly irrational. In one sense this is true: it reflects flawed reasoning. But, in the Stoic view, it is reasoning, all the same. Seneca explains that emotions are elicited, in the first instance, by impressions and then judged to be genuine or not by the mind. As he explains in *On Anger*: "There is no doubt but that what arouses anger is the impression that is presented of an offense." This account recalls Aristotle's, and Seneca indeed affirms that "Aristotle's definition is not far from ours."

For the Stoics, however, the mere response to an impression— the shock—is not yet anger, but a preliminary step. Imagine I am standing at a street corner, and someone suddenly shoves me from behind. My instinctive reaction might be anger: How dare he? But note that this response requires making an assumption about the motive of the offender. Suppose it turns out that I was standing in the path of an oncoming bicycle, and the shove in fact saved me from harm. I might now feel gratitude, perhaps, or relief, but surely no longer anger. There may be a residue of tension, as a result of the initial shock; but this purely physical reaction is not, properly speaking, an emotion.

Seneca describes a class of feelings that, he says, are not emotions in the strict sense but rather "the initial preliminaries to emotions." He provides a lengthy and, at first blush, rather puzzling list of these proto-emotions, including such responses as shivering or goose pimples when one is sprinkled with cold water, aversion to certain kinds of touch, and the vertigo we experience when we look down from great heights. But he also mentions our reaction to spectacles in the theater, historical narratives, and paintings of horrible things, as well as the sight of punishments (even when they are deserved) and contagious laughter and sadness. These motions are irresistible; they "do not arise through our will" and thus do not yield to reason.

A genuine emotion, on the other hand, involves a judgment, or rather two. As Seneca says, Stoics

> maintain that anger does not venture anything on its own but only when the mind approves; for to accept the impression of an injury that has been sustained and desire vengeance for it—and to unite the two judgments, that one ought not to have been harmed and that one ought to be avenged—this is not characteristic of an impulse that is aroused without our will.

Anger, then, requires that "one has discerned something, grown indignant, condemned it, and takes revenge." This distinction—that the mind consents to the reasons for anger—is crucial, because, as Seneca explains, if anger "arises in us without our willing it, it will never submit to reason," and philosophy will have no therapeutic value.

Anger, then, is voluntary, insofar as it depends on our assent to the proposition that we have been harmed and that revenge is warranted. But once anger takes over, things change. For, as Seneca argues, reason retains its authority only as long as it is separated from the emotions; once it mixes with them, reason is helpless. The mind, in the Stoic view, has no separate place of its own, and once it is transformed by an emotion, it can no longer free itself. When people are wholly in the grip of anger, for example, they are unresponsive to reason, and the only way they can be discouraged from taking revenge is if their rage is displaced by some other emotion. As Seneca observes, this is hardly a reliable way to curb a passion, and it runs counter to the Stoic condemnation of emotions generally. Far from Aristotle's notion that an inability to feel anger is servile, Seneca sees anger as a violent master, one that holds us in thrall.

It should be noted here that Seneca, who was a tutor for the emperor Nero, was forced to kill himself for allegedly conspiring in a plot to kill the emperor. Indeed, the new, more cautious attitude toward anger represented, in part, a generalized anxiety among the upper classes who were themselves vulnerable to the rage of their superiors, as Seneca was to Nero's. By the second century CE, the great doctor Galen was describing anger as "a sickness of the soul." In his treatise *On the Passions and Errors of the Soul*, Galen records various anecdotes illustrating the perils of unrestrained rage:

> When I was still a youth and pursuing this training, I watched a man eagerly trying to open a door. When things did not work out as he would have them, I saw him bite the key, kick the door, blaspheme, glare wildly like a madman, and all but foam at the mouth like a wild boar. When I saw this, I conceived such a hatred for anger that I was never thereafter seen behaving in an unseemly manner because of it.

Galen also recollects his mother's fits of temper, saying she "was so very prone to anger that sometimes she bit her handmaids; she constantly shrieked at my father and fought with him." Then as now, anger would have manifested itself differently according to class, gender, ethnic background, and other variables, not to mention strictly individual differences. But the broad outlines of these examples from antiquity are instructive as they increasingly shift the perspective from those who feel wronged to the perspective of the helpless victims and the trivial oversights that elicit the violence of enraged masters.

ANOTHER HISTORICAL INFLECTION of anger arrived in the second century CE as Christianity spread through the Roman Empire, culminating in the conversion of the emperor Constantine around 312. The Bible made it clear that God could be wrathful, and Christian writers were confronted with the task of rehabilitating this emotion, so roundly condemned by the Stoics. There must be a right way to be wrathful, they thought. Thus Tertullian, writing early in the third century, affirms God will indeed grow angry, but "he will do so rationally, at those with whom he ought to be."

Lactantius, an advisor to Constantine, made a similar move. In his essay *On the Anger of God*, he notes the Stoic view that God possesses *gratia* or "grace" but not anger, since anger is a reaction to harm (to which God is not vulnerable) and takes the form of a perturbation of the mind (which is foreign to God's nature). Lactantius replies, however, that if God is not angry at the impious and unjust, neither can he love the pious and just; for as he loves the good, he hates those who are evil. The two emotions, anger and love, are necessarily paired, and one can no more exist without the other than right can exist without left. There is a just anger and an unjust anger.

When Seneca, agreeing with Aristotle, speaks of anger as a desire for revenge, he is referring, Lactantius explains, to the unjust kind of anger; proper anger seeks rather to correct wickedness. The great Cappadocian theologian Basil of Caesarea expresses a similar view in his *Homily Against Those Who Are Angry*: "For if you are not angry at the Evil One, it is impossible for you to hate him as much as he deserves. For it is necessary, I believe, to have equal zeal in regard to the love of virtue and the hatred of sin, and for this anger is most useful."

On this account, a good king was not one who had eliminated anger, as Seneca argues. On the contrary, such a disposition signaled a lack of righteous will. As Stephen White observed in Barbara Rosenwein's collection *Anger's Past: The Social Uses of an Emotion in the Middle Ages* (1998), "Whether or not displays of lordly anger express what we would recognize as anger, they were gestures of a feuding culture." White cites the example of Henry I, who in a rage punished the traitorous Conan without even giving him the chance to confess his sins: "Henry, stern avenger of his brother's injury, trembled with rage and, scorning the wretch's prayers, thrust him violently with both hands, hurling him down from the window of the tower."

No age is monolithic, of course, and there were Christians who were profoundly opposed to the idea that God could be the bearer of any human emotions, much less one so violent as anger. The first-century Jewish thinker Philo of Alexandria had already denied, in his work *That God Is Immutable*, that references to God's passions in the Bible were to be taken literally. If Jesus wept for Lazarus, some argued that it was *as though* out of grief. The monk and theologian John Cassian maintained in his *Conferences* that the "disease of anger must be utterly rooted out of the recesses of our soul." Cassian knew that some defended human anger on the grounds that "God himself is said to be furious and angry with those who either are unwilling to know him, or, though they do know him, scorn him." But Cassian denounces this view as "a most abominable interpretation of the Scriptures," on a par with supposing that God sleeps or sits or has a body similar to that of human beings. Rather than understanding mentions of God's anger as referring to the human passion, Cassian urged, one must realize that God is "a stranger to every perturbation." As Cassian and many others since have reasoned, the ascription of anger to God is a way of inspiring fear of offending him, but does not imply that his judgments are motivated by some just and pure version of the emotion.

LET US TAKE STOCK of the transformation we have charted. In the face of insult or injustice, Aristotle found it demeaning to demonstrate meekness or humility. Three hundred years later, Jesus recommended turning the other cheek. These and other interpretations of anger continue to be manifested in the way we think and feel now. Is anger a desire for revenge, a product of false reasoning, a form of righteous indignation, or foreign to the nature of God and the wise ruler?

Today there is an entire industry devoted to anger management, which commonly treats anger as an irrational impulse needing to be controlled or repressed. Others have encouraged anger, regarding its repression as a technique by which the oppressed are kept in their place. Donald Trump, for his part, is at the center of conflicting views about anger. In headline after headline his anger is said to "boil over," reflecting a hydraulic image of emotion, and he is accused of fueling the anger of his base, like a flame destined to catch on in deadly fashion. But Trump also causes anger and stress in his opponents, and many on the political left are angry about his policies.

This complex repertoire of rage is not atavistic, and it is not new; these are the shapes that anger has taken, in its multiple dimensions, and it is not always regarded, felt, or understood in the same ways. A historical perspective does not allow us to adjudicate when and whether anger is due, or what form it should take. But it may help to clarify our sentiments, and that is a good beginning.

VICTIM ANGER AND ITS COSTS
Martha C. Nussbaum

Thus did every type of bad practice take root in Greece, fed by these civil wars. Openness, which is the largest part of noble character, was laughed down; it vanished. Mistrustful opposition of spirit carried the day, destroying all trust. To reconcile them no speech was strong enough, no oath fearful enough. All of them alike, when they got the upper hand, calculating that security was not to be hoped for, became more intent on self-protection than they were capable of trust.

—Thucydides, *The Peloponnesian Wars*

Hecuba's Transformation

IT IS THE END of the Trojan War. Hecuba, the noble queen of Troy, has endured many losses: her husband, her children, her fatherland, destroyed by fire. And yet she remains an admirable person—loving, capable of trust and friendship, combining autonomous action with extensive concern for others. But then she suffers a betrayal that cuts deep, traumatizing her entire personality. A close friend, Polymestor, to whom she has entrusted the care of her last remaining child, murders the child for money. That is the central event in Euripides's *Hecuba* (424 BCE), an anomalous version of the Trojan war story, shocking in its moral ugliness, and yet one of the most insightful dramas in the tragic canon.

From the moment Hecuba learns of Polymestor's betrayal, she is a different person. Unable to repose any trust in anyone, unwilling to be persuaded, she becomes utterly solipsistic and dedicates herself entirely to revenge. She murders Polymestor's children and puts out his eyes—symbolizing, it would seem, the total extinction of their relationship of mutuality and care, as well as her own refusal of friendly reciprocal vision. Polymestor wanders onstage blind, crawling on all fours like the beast he always was. At the end of the play, it is prophesied that Hecuba will be transformed into a dog—an animal the Greeks (wrongly) associated with rabid pursuit of prey and a total lack of interpersonal concern. As Dante summarizes her story in the *Inferno*, "deranged, she barked like a dog: so far had anguish twisted her mind."

Hecuba is not just grief-stricken: she is stricken, as well, in the very core of her moral personality. She can no longer sustain virtues that used to define her as a human being, friend, and citizen. In depicting her transformation, Euripides clearly inverts the mythic creation of citizenship and human community depicted in the final drama of Aeschylus's *Oresteia* (458 BCE), by then a famous creation story of the Athenian democracy. Initially the Furies, grim goddesses of revenge, are said to be like dogs, sniffing after their prey, incapable of love or justice. But at the end of the play, they agree to trust the promises of goddess Athena and to adopt a new way of thinking characterized by "mildness of temper" and "a mindset of communal friendship." They stand up, receive the robes of adult citizens, and celebrate the law-abiding justice of the city.

Aeschylus's moral is that a political community must abandon the obsessive pursuit of revenge and adopt an idea of justice that is both law-governed and welfare-oriented, focusing not on hunting one's prey but on deterring bad behavior and producing prosperity. For Euripides, however, moral trauma can cause the collapse of trust and the other-regarding virtues, producing a revenge-obsessed parody of real justice.

Euripides's grim drama is part of a long tradition of reflection, in the Greco-Roman world, about the damage that events beyond people's own control can do to them as they aim to lead a flourishing human life, a life that includes acting in accordance with all the major virtues. The most prominent conclusion of this tradition is that events people don't control can block them from acting in socially valuable ways. By removing political citizenship, friends, family, and the wherewithal to act in society, such events may prevent a person from living a completely flourishing life, what the Greeks called *eudaimonia*. Just having the virtues inside, as Aristotle and others stress, is not enough, if one is radically cut off from acting. But *Hecuba* suggests a more radical conclusion: such events can also corrode the virtues themselves, producing moral damage of a long-standing sort. The first sort of damage can be reversed: an exiled person can be restored to citizenship, the friendless can acquire new friends. But Hecuba's damage lies deeper, in longstanding patterns of action and aspiration that form part of her character. Particularly vulnerable are the relational virtues, patterns of friendship and trust. Bad treatment at the hands of others—experiencing a violation of trust—can make people worse.

How can this be? How can the crimes of Polymestor undermine Hecuba's virtue? Aristotle appears to deny the possibility, holding that a good person will be firm in character and will "always do the finest thing possible given the circumstances," amid the blows of fortune, although perhaps, in extreme circumstances, falling short of full *eudaimonia*. Most tragic dramas agree, portraying heroes and heroines who remain noble under fortune's blows. The character Hecuba in Euripides's play *The Trojan Women* is just such a noble figure, showing love, leadership, and the capacity for rational deliberation in the midst of disaster. His *Hecuba*, virtually unique in the Greek tragic corpus, depicts tragic events in all their potential ugliness, showing us that their cost is often greater than our stories reveal. For this reason, the play has been valued low through most of the modern era, dismissed as repugnant and a mere horror show. As scholar Ernst Abramson observed in 1952, it came to the fore again in the light of the grim events of the twentieth century, which have shown that good character is more fragile than we like to think.

Immutable Virtue?

IT IS ATTRACTIVE for feminists to believe that victims are always pure and right—women and other victims of injustice. Often they are inspired by a prevalent modern philosophical view: the good will is not affected by contingencies beyond people's control. Immanuel Kant is one of the most influential sources for this view, although it has ancient Greco-Roman antecedents in Stoic ethics (which influenced both Christian ethics and Kant), and it also corresponds to some strands within Christian thought. Kant says in the *Groundwork for the Metaphysics of Morals* (1785) that even if the good will has no chance at all to accomplish anything, "yet would it, like a jewel, still shine by its own light as something which has its full value in itself. Its usefulness or fruitlessness can neither augment nor diminish this value." The jewel image clearly implies, further, that the will cannot be corrupted by those same external circumstances. People who hold this view may also be inspired by a well-known psychological tendency known as the "just world" hypothesis: if there is misery, it must be deserved. If no desert, no deep harm.

Early in the feminist tradition, the Kantian view was called into question. Mary Wollstonecraft analyzed the damage women's personalities and aspirations suffer under inequality. She claimed that women all too often exhibit servility, emotional lack of control, and lack of due regard for their own rationality and autonomy. These, she argued, are morally bad traits that women have been nudged into by their dependence on the good will of men. Criticizing Jean-Jacques Rousseau, who praised the coy and submissive Sophie as a norm for female character, she insisted that women, just as much as men, should have the opportunity to grow into fully autonomous agents, winning self-respect and the respect of others for their dignity and self-authored choices. When they are denied this opportunity, they suffer damage at the very core of their being.

In a similar vein, John Stuart Mill insisted in *The Subjection of Women* (1869) that one of the worst aspects of the male "subjection" of women is its mental and moral aspect:

> Men do not want solely the obedience of women, they want their senti-
> ments. All men, except the most brutish, desire to have, in the woman
> most nearly connected with them, not a forced slave but a willing one,
> not a slave merely, but a favorite. They have therefore put everything in
> practice to enslave their minds. The masters of all other slaves rely, for
> maintaining obedience, on fear: either fear of themselves, or religious fears.
> The masters of women wanted more than simple obedience, and they
> turned the whole force of education to effect their purpose. All women
> are brought up from the very earliest years in the belief that their ideal of
> character is the very opposite to that of men; not self-will, and government
> by self-control, but submission, and yielding to the control of others.

Because women are brought up this way, and because, in their socially and legally powerless condition, they cannot obtain anything
except by pleasing men, women think that being attractive to men
is the main thing in life.

> And, this great means of influence over the minds of women having
> been acquired, an instinct of selfishness made men avail themselves
> of it to the utmost as a means of holding women in subjection, by
> representing to them meekness, submissiveness, and resignation of
> all individual will into the hands of a man, as an essential part of
> sexual attractiveness.

These insightful observations have been taken up in recent times by
social scientists working on the deformation of preferences under

conditions of inequality. Jon Elster's *Sour Grapes* (1983) used the idea of "adaptive preferences" to explain the long persistence of feudalism, and the fact that the revolutions of the eighteenth century required a revolution in consciousness before a change in rights could be achieved. Elster took his title from Aesop's fable in which a fox, learning quickly that the grapes he initially wants are out of reach for him, quickly schools himself not to want them and calls them "sour." Other scholars working on these phenomena have emphasized that deformed preferences can be found even earlier in life, so that people learn never to want the attractive thing in the first place—thus echoing Wollstonecraft's and Mill's observations about women. Economist Amartya Sen has found deformed preferences in subordinated women even where their own physical strength and health is concerned. I have developed the same idea in connection with preferences about higher education and political participation.

But modern feminists have some strong reasons for sticking to the Kantian view. Victim-blaming is ubiquitous as a strategy of subordination. It comes easy to the proud to construct fictions of their own moral superiority, portraying the subordinated as in some sense deserving their subordination because of intellectual and moral inferiority. Colonial domination was typically "justified" by arguments alleging that the dominated people are like children, needing firm control. Even the usually clear-eyed Mill said this about the people and cultures of India (while in the employ of the British East India Company). In our own time we have all heard such denigrations of African Americans and African American culture as excuses for white dominance: the black family is allegedly morally inferior to the white family, black culture to white culture. Indeed such victim-blaming is a virtual trope of recent conservative thought about race. As philosopher Lisa Tessman says of one such critic in *Burdened Virtues* (2005), "His account leaves no space for implicating the oppressive social systems that cause moral damage." A substantial feminist literature raises doubts about the concept of adaptive preferences as applied to women, for similar reasons. There is no subordinated group that has not been systematically charged with preexisting moral deficiency—charges that deny the extent of damage that domination does to the subordinated.

It seems crucial for people seeking justice to face these grim facts and their moral toll. There are delicate issues here: Up to what point is social damage merely a source of unhappiness, and at what point does it eat into the moral personality? How far do subordinated peoples really internalize and act out the negative image of themselves purveyed by their dominators, thus—as Wollstonecraft and Mill argue—failing to achieve key moral virtues? One must approach the complexity of these issues subtly and yet frankly. It does no good to pretend that everything is rosy when people are schooled to servility and deprived of encouragement for autonomy. Indeed such a pretense plays into the hands of dominators by implying that what they have done is merely superficial.

In general, here's how the world looks to me. First, dominators usually have a defective moral culture that rationalizes their domination in many ways, not least by its victim blaming. Second, one thing they typically do in order to maintain their power is to encourage servility and an absence of autonomy and courage in the subjugated. They also inflict trauma by cruelty, one purpose of which is to break victims' spirit. Sometimes they fail: people have great resources of resilience and insight, and can indeed shine like jewels in the worst of circumstances. But sometimes they succeed, and that success is the dominators' deepest moral crime.

Women are especially likely to exhibit a complicated mixture of moral overcoming and moral damage. Unlike most subordinated groups, they live in intimate proximity to their dominators. This is good for them in a way, since it means that they may be well fed, cared for, even educated. But it is also bad for them: the intimate context contains depths of cruelty that are not always present outside of intimacy, and needs for boundless submission on the part of the thirsty proud. In a 1980 essay in *Ethics* entitled "Racism and Sexism," African American philosopher Laurence Thomas predicted that sexism would prove more difficult to eradicate than racism, because males had a stake in the domination of women (expressed, for example, in the phrase "a real man") that whites do not typically have in the domination of blacks (no parallel phrase "a real white," or so he said). Thomas's article received a lot of sharp critiques, and, forty years later, it does seem that he is wrong about the depth of racism in U.S. culture. What he said, however, is surely true of sexual orientation prejudice as compared with sexism in U.S. society. Sexual orientation prejudice has dropped away with startling rapidity—in part because dominant straight society has no stake in it. There is no concept of the "real straight" that entails ongoing subordination of LGBTQ people. With gender, given the usually intimate context, the stake males have in producing pliant women remains high.

Moral Damage in Feminist Thought

FEMINIST PHILOSOPHERS have not typically been uncritical Kantians. Kant and white male Kantians did not need to wrestle with sexual violence, domination by a spouse, or the myriad problems that child care and domestic work pose for women's aspirations. They, and their twentieth-century followers, casually asserted things about virtue that were false: for example, that two valid moral claims could never conflict. One way that luck influences virtue, as the Greek tragic poets knew well, is precisely by producing such conflicts, in which it seems that whatever one does, one will be slighting the claims of some important commitment or virtue. Kant simply denied that this ever happened, and many followed him.

Female philosophers of my generation questioned that denial. Juggling child care and work, we knew that circumstances beyond good people's control often produced painful contingent moral conflicts, particularly in an unjust society. We had allies among leading male philosophers—particularly Bernard Williams (who actually did a lot of child care and, in general, understood women's demands with a rare sensitivity). But it was far more difficult for powerless young women to make bold countercultural claims than for a dominant male, who had, in addition, served as an Royal Air Force pilot during his national service.

We did persist, however. And although outstanding female philosophers have worked in the Kantian tradition (often showing its complexities and tensions)—women such as Onora O'Neill, Christine Korsgaard, Barbara Herman, Marcia Baron, and Nancy Sherman (also an Aristotelian)—on the whole, women doing explicitly feminist philosophy have rarely been Kantians, because they have felt that Kant denied truths of their experience. Barbara Herman did show surprisingly, and cogently, that Kant has important insights about the urge for domination inherent in sexual relations. But hers was a late attempt to show feminists who had dismissed Kant that he actually had something to offer them, as indeed he does. My own approach to the topic of objectification is infused with Kantian ideas, and I have learned a lot from the views of Herman and Korsgaard—as well as, of course, the great (Kant-inspired) John Rawls. For the most part, however, feminist philosophers have been drawn to other sources and have used other insights to craft views that take the damages of domination seriously.

A pioneer in this area was Sandra Bartky. Already in 1984, in her essay "Feminine Masochism and the Politics of Personal Transformation," she insisted—as had Wollstonecraft before her—that many of women's emotions and character traits have been shaped by a system of domination to serve its ends. She insisted that views that deny the possibility of such damage are highly superficial:

> Those who claim that any woman can reprogram her consciousness if only she is sufficiently determined hold a shallow view of the nature of patriarchal oppression. Anything done can be undone, it is implied; nothing has been permanently damaged, nothing irretrievably lost. But this is tragically false. One of the evils of a system of oppression is that it may damage people in ways that cannot always be undone.

In another valuable essay, "Foucault, Femininity, and the Modernization of Patriarchal Power," she described—echoing Mill, but with far greater specificity—the production of an "ideal body of femininity" that serves male interests, being slender rather than massive, weak rather than muscular. I would add that this was written when women were forbidden to run in marathons on the grounds that this would tax their frail reproductive organs, and in which female tennis players were upbraided for looking muscular. (Chrissie Evert represented the "good" woman, Martina Navratilova, who introduced serious weight training to the tennis regimen, the "bad" woman.)

My own work on "moral luck," in *The Fragility of Goodness* (1986), was not explicitly feminist, but was inspired both by life and by discussions with other women. And valuable work on moral luck began to crop up all over the profession. Claudia Card took aim at the ideal of women as caring helpmeets in the work of such people as Carol Gilligan and Nel Noddings. Making eloquent use of Friedrich Nietzsche, she argued that the valorization of self-abnegation is a kind of slave morality: women, feeling themselves powerless, give the name of virtue to traits that powerlessness has imposed upon us. (Related insights were developed already in 1973 by a male Kantian, Thomas Hill, in an important essay, "Servility and Self-Respect," which explicitly alludes to the way a male-dominated society requires servile behavior of women.)

In a related vein, Marcia Homiak, a distinguished Aristotle scholar, argued in a series of articles that real virtue requires enjoyment of one's own activity and a type of "rational self-love" cultivated in confident relationships with others—and that sexism has all too often robbed women of that joy and that confidence. Her insights have been too little heralded, and feminists should make them central.

In 2005 Tessman contributed an important systematic study on the whole phenomenon of moral damage in the context of feminist struggle and resistance. Following the example of those who draw on ancient Greek thought, but with valuable contemporary elaboration, Tessman argues in *Burdened Virtues* that in a variety of ways sexism damages the subordinated self. She concludes that thinking seriously about equality means thinking, as well, about the need to repair the damaged self, supporting the cultivation of virtues that domination has made difficult.

Thinkers in this tradition can still stress, as many do, that we must listen to the narratives of victims and give their account of their own experience some degree of priority. That epistemic correction is important, since members of subordinated groups have typically been denied an equal status as knowers and givers of testimony. Listening never means listening with no critical questions, and the possibility that moral damage is distorting the narrative—often in an "adaptive" direction, denying real wrongs—ought to be with us always as we listen.

Is Retributivism a "Burdened Virtue"?

TESSMAN MAKES a further valuable point about the virtues. The struggle against systematic wrongdoing, she argues, requires a specific battery of traits that may be virtuous in the context of the struggle—advancing its goals—but not as elements in the life of an agent striving to live well. A type of uncritical loyalty and solidarity, for example, may be required in a political struggle, and yet it may not equip us for the best, most reciprocal types of friendship. We can think of many further cases.

Consider two cases, closely related, that point us back to Euripides's play. The first is the denial of trust and friendship to those on the "other side." The second is a focus on retributive anger. Tessman explicitly remarks on the latter: she says that this type of victim anger is useful to the political struggle, but that it can also become excessive and obsessive, deforming the self. So people have a tragic choice before them: either fail to fit oneself maximally for struggle, or do so, but lose some of the richness of a fully virtuous personality.

I agree with Tessman that in both of the cases I have named there is distortion of the personality, but I don't agree that this distortion is useful for a liberatory struggle. We don't have a tragic choice after all, although we do have the extremely difficult task of waging a difficult struggle without poisoned weapons. If we want reconciliation and a shared future in the long run, we had better figure out how not to slip into burdened so-called virtues.

Let's think first of mistrust of all people on the "other side." Hecuba learned only that Polymestor was untrustworthy, but she concluded that all men are untrustworthy. This is a common move in feminism (as in other struggles for equality). In my time, heterosexual women were often charged with disloyalty to the feminist cause, and the phrase "woman-oriented woman" was used to mean both "feminist" and "lesbian." Some otherwise admirable feminist groups also advised their members not to collaborate professionally with males. (The same tendency can be found in other movements for equality.)

I gave my book chapter on *Hecuba* as a Eunice Belgum Memorial Lecture after her tragic suicide. A gifted PhD classmate of mine, Eunice had gotten a good job at a liberal arts college. Once there, she co-taught a class on feminism with a male (feminist) faculty member. At a meeting of the Society for Women in Philosophy (SWIP), of which Eunice was a member, she was denounced for betraying the cause by cooperating with a male faculty member. Her parents told me that she made many phone calls the day she committed suicide, including to female students in her class to apologize for corrupting their consciousness by trusting a male faculty member. I felt and feel that Eunice was (originally) correct and that SWIP was wrong. If we can't form carefully sifted cooperations with well-intentioned people on the "other side," we have no hope of eventual reconciliation. Thus the refusal of trust is not a "burdened virtue" in Tessman's sense: it is not useful, and it retards the progress of the struggle.

Indeed, sometimes a struggle requires trust even without solid evidence of intentions. Nelson Mandela was no credulous weakling. His ability to trust others was combined with a secure and advanced critical capacity. Throughout the struggle in South Africa, he formed close bonds with white allies (including Denis Goldberg, a Rivonia codefendant, and Albie Sachs, later a distinguished judge). These friendships were carefully sifted over the years, partly through Mandela's close ties to the South African Jewish community. Here, trust was well founded. But Mandela also took some risks in the trust department. During coverage of his funeral in 2013, I remember seeing a middle-aged policeman recall, with tears in his eyes, a moment during Mandela's inaugural parade as president in 1994.

Nussbaum

Mandela got down from his car to talk to a group of young police recruits, all white as of course they were. He shook their hands and said, "Our trust is in you. Our trust is in you." They had expected only hostility and retribution from Mandela, and he offered them his trust. In this case, unlike those of Sachs, Goldberg, and so many others, the trust had not been earned or scrutinized. But the men were young and malleable, and Mandela proposed to leverage friendship and trustworthiness by behaving in a friendly and trusting manner. I think this is the right direction for us all. The *Hecuba* reminds us that, without trust (which is never perfectly secure), there is no hope of community.

Let's now think about anger. The feminist case for anger imagines anger as vigorous protest, the opposite of servile inactivity. As such, anger looks strong, indeed essential. However, we must begin by making a distinction. If we analyze anger into its component parts, as a long philosophical tradition in both Western and non-Western thought has done, it includes: pain at a perceived wrongful act that is thought to have affected the angry person, or some people or causes she cares a lot about. Here we already have lots of room for error: the person may be wrong about whether the act was wrongfully inflicted rather than just accidentally; she may be wrong about its significance. But let's suppose that these thoughts withstand scrutiny: then anger (thus far) is an appropriate response to wrongdoing. It expresses a demand: this is wrong, and it should not happen again. It alludes to the past, but it faces forward and proposes to fix the world going into the future.

This is the type of anger that I have called transition anger, because it registers something that has already happened, but turns to the future for a remedy. This type of anger may be accompanied by proposals to punish the offender, but these proposals will understand punishment in one or more future-directed ways: as reform, as expression of important norms, as "specific deterrence" for that same offender, and as "general deterrence" for other offenders contemplating similar crimes.

Transition anger is indeed important for a struggle against injustice. It is outraged protest, and protest is important to draw attention to the wrong and energize people to address it. Nor does this type of anger "burden" the personality. It is exhilarating and liberating to face forward and imagine solutions to problems. Nor does this type of anger risk becoming obsessive or distorted.

However, let's face it: this is not all that people usually mean by anger. Anger is rarely pure of a further element (present in all the philosophical definitions of anger I know, including Gandhi's): the wish for payback, for commensurate pain to befall the aggressor. I've already said that transition anger can give a useful role to punishment, so it's tricky to distinguish the future-directed type from the purely back-directed retributive type. But people are usually not pure in their orientation to future welfare. When struck, their impulse is to strike back. They so easily imagine that a counterbalancing pain on the other side annuls or undoes their pain or wrong. Hence the widespread support for capital punishment among relatives of homicide victims. Capital punishment has never been shown to have deterrent value. People call for it because of its alleged proportional retributive fittingness. Your child's death is made good by the criminal's death, or so it is all too easy to think.

We all know victims who focus obsessively on retributive fantasies and plans toward those who have wronged them. Virtually the entirety of divorce and child custody litigation is retributive in spirit, rarely aimed at equity and general welfare. Our major religions nourish retributive fantasies: the book of Revelation, for example, deserves Nietzsche's judgment that it is an ugly revenge fantasy. And a study of the way "victim impact" statements have figured in criminal trials shows that they serve largely to ramp up the demand for harsh punishment of a retributive sort. Past injuries, however, are past. Pain creates more pain and does not repair the original injury. The proportionality of pain to past pain is, by itself, never a reason for a harsh punishment, and it typically distracts from the task of fixing the future.

Both Western and Indian philosophical traditions (the only non-Western ones I know enough about to speak) judge that ordinary anger is retributive; what I have called transition anger is exceptional. Studying the breakdown of marriages and friendships, one is inclined to agree. However, the numbers don't matter: it is the distinction that matters, and this distinction has simply not been clearly made, throughout the whole philosophical tradition. Transition anger is useful in a struggle and does not burden the personality. Retributive anger burdens the personality—and is not very useful in a struggle for freedom. Martin Luther King, Jr., the one distinguished Western philosopher who did recognize and emphasize this distinction, spoke of the way that the anger of people in his movement had to be purified and "channelized." In a statement in 1959, he vividly characterized the two types.

One is the development of a wholesome social organization to resist with effective, firm measures any efforts to impede progress. The other is a confused, anger-motivated drive to strike back violently, to inflict damage. Primarily, it seeks to cause injury to retaliate for wrongful suffering. . . . It is punitive—not radical or constructive.

I'm with King: the retaliatory sort is not useful to the struggle because it is confused and not constructive. Nor is it really "radical" in the sense of creating something new and better. King wanted accountability, legal punishment, and the public expression of shared values. He rejected pain for pain as easy, weak, and stupid.

The Weakness of the Furies

FEMINISM TODAY needs a similar distinction. Anger is strong and valuable if it expresses well-grounded outrage and faces forward—with constructive ideas, a refusal of payback retributivism, and, let's hope, a radical trust in what we may create by joining together. It is not strong and valuable if it indulges in easy retributivism, and we all know that getting stuck in retributivism is a common human weakness. If we see clearly the weakness of retributivism in the capital punishment context—and I believe most feminists do see that—it seems odd to defend retributivism as essential to feminist struggle. Strangely, however, even when the distinction between retributive anger and what I call transition anger has been announced and made central, as it was by King and as others have done in his spirit

Nussbaum

more recently, feminist discussions of anger's value tends to ignore the distinction and ride roughshod over it—so hard it is to get one's mind around the fact that there is an anger that eschews retribution.

We need to address the future, and for that we need an uncertain trust and a radical type of love.

WHOSE ANGER COUNTS?
Whitney Phillips

I RECENTLY SPOKE with a reporter about the legacy of Gamergate, a hate and harassment campaign directed at women and people of color in the gaming and tech industries. The offensive, which began in 2014 and lingered for years, was a nightmare for those targeted, sending some women fleeing from their homes out of fear for their physical safety. The threats weren't just credible, they weren't just terrifying; they were incessant, sometimes targeting family members as well. Gamergate continues to be a nightmare for many. Just talking about it can subject a person to new waves of abuse and harassment.

I explained this history to the reporter. Gamergate was far from an isolated, past-tense event, I said; it is an ongoing pattern and behavioral template. You can't understand the rise of the reactionary far right since the 2016 election without understanding where and how those energies emerged. Nor can you separate the tactics used by Gamergate participants in 2014 from the tactics used by white supremacists in 2019. These include brigading (swarming a person with abuse) and doxing (publicizing private information to facilitate even more abuse), both of which remain common practices within far-right circles.

After I explained all this, there was a pause on the other end of the phone.

"Don't you think," the reporter asked, "that there's a similar energy on the other side?"

I asked them to clarify.

"People on the other side," the reporter continued. "Canceling people, attacking them for the things they say on Twitter? Calling their bosses, getting them fired? Wouldn't you say it's the same kind of thing?"

When I followed up again, the reporter specified even further: they weren't just talking about attacks against everyday people. They were suggesting that the violence done during Gamergate was the same as pushback against the very kinds of people responsible for Gamergate.

Given the focus of our discussion, and all the horrors I'd just laid out, I was taken aback. But I can't say I was terribly surprised; this wasn't the first time a reporter had asked me this type of question. I've seen similar assertions made even more frequently in news articles, on cable television, and screamed across social media.

Sometimes the equivocation between bigots on the right and cancel or call-out culture on the left—which tends to align with anti-racist activism, intersectional feminism, and other social justice efforts—is explicit. People say, directly, that "both sides" are responsible for the chaos roaring through our politics. Other times, the equal sign is implicit. Yes, we have a problem with white supremacy or misogyny, this argument goes, and that's a special kind of bad. But all the social justice warrioring happening on the left is out of control. Cancel culture, often cited as yet more evidence of "PC culture run amok," is accused of undermining the progressive cause and, ultimately, benefiting racists by equating violence with poorly chosen words, providing "real" racists a convenient smokescreen.

Still other times, the comparison between violent reactionaries and social justice pushback is more subtle. In these cases, cancel culture is denounced as the reason we can't have nice things on-line, while bigoted violence is omitted from the discussion entirely. Presumably, bigots still exist in this narrative universe, and are unwelcome figures. But when the focus of all the hand-wringing is on the people pushing back against bigots, the threat level of cancel culture gets unnecessarily elevated. In a *New York Times* op-ed, for example, David Brooks illustrates how quickly this argument can escalate, suggesting that "The Cruelty of Call-Out Culture" has "taken a step toward the Rwandan genocide."

Any equivalence, implicit or explicit, between the push for justice and reactionary violence is false. This isn't a claim about what specific tactics are used on either side. A hateful message and a supportive message could both be written on a piece of paper in pencil; no one would say the messages were the same, simply because the tool was the same.

Similarly, regardless of what tactics might be used, terrorizing, dehumanizing, and endangering someone because of how they were born is a different thing, with different power dynamics and different consequences, than efforts to confront hate. Hate is a source of injustice; it punishes its targets for existing. Confronting hate is a response to injustice; it punishes its targets for making it more difficult for marginalized people to exist. There is, without question, room to critique how social justice efforts unfold in particular cases. But punching a Nazi isn't the same as being a Nazi. Those on the progressive left and reactionary right should be analyzed and historicized separately.

The false equivalency between social justice activists and reactionaries doesn't just obscure the fact that they're doing categorically different things. It also obscures the divergent rules and expectations social justice activists and reactionaries are subjected to, particularly around the expression of anger. In other words, it is not just that their actions aren't equivalent; they also aren't *treated* equally. The anger of those seeking justice—especially those who are black, brown, female, or members of other minority groups—is minimized, pathologized, and knee-jerk condemned. By contrast, the anger of those enacting injustice against those very bodies—who tend to be white, frequently male, and members of dominant groups—is taken seriously, placed in context, and very often granted a path to redemption.

THE PATHOLOGIZING OF CANCEL CULTURE begins with the name itself. For those who criticize the practice, the term "cancel culture" is especially fitting; it represents the dangers of being caught in the eye of the online storm. At any moment, for any reason, the mob will strike, erasing people—maybe even you!—for the slightest mistakes.

It is certainly true that collective pushback efforts can get out of hand, or emerge from a misunderstanding, or even be manufactured by far-right instigators to sow chaos and confusion on the left. It is also true that some people pile on for the sake of piling on; they repeat calls for cancelation not because of a strong ideological conviction, but because being a member of the in-group is preferable to being labeled as one of "them." Each case is different; some instances warrant strong critique, and so do some people.

That said, broadly condemning all instances of call-out and cancellation—in some cases, equivocating between ideologically motivated critique and people simply being mean to each other—obscures the root of the problem. Collective intervention is very often the only available channel for dissent, because social accountability is so frequently denied those targeted by bigotry and other forms of identity-based violence. Sarah Hagi emphasizes this point, arguing in *Time* that the angry mob caricature of cancel culture gets the issue all wrong. What's actually happening, she argues, is a move toward public accountability. Thanks to social media, marginalized people now have public channels for pushing back against the powerful. "This applies to not only wealthy people or industry leaders," Hagi explains, "but anyone whose privilege has historically shielded them from public scrutiny. Because they can't handle this cultural shift, they rely on phrases like 'cancel culture' to delegitimize the criticism."

And there's a lot to criticize, online and off. Examples of unchecked injustice are everywhere. They are the Jeffrey Epsteins and Harvey Weinsteins, who continue abusing and raping and exploiting with impunity with the backing—even the blessing—of powerful institutions. They are the everyday acts of violence—online and off, professional and personal, big and small—directed at trans and indigenous and immigrant and black and brown bodies, and framed as that person's fault, or not fully investigated, or merely ignored by those who take their own embodied safety for granted. They are the hugs and calls for forgiveness when the perpetrator is white and is believed to have a promising future, or is seen as deserving the benefit of the doubt. They are the people who have done wrong, and should face consequences, yet barely experience a hiatus, let alone a cancellation.

The policies of companies such as Facebook and Twitter all but guarantee this last outcome. In doing so, they point to a facet of the debate that is rarely discussed. While the equivalence between justice and reactionary violence doesn't hold up, there is another, less obvious equivalency that does: the equally destructive effects of the reactionaries themselves and the social media companies that aid, abet, and normalize them. These companies have long privileged the experiences of abusers, antagonists, and bigots over the people these groups target, who are either sacrificed in the name of "free speech" (or maximizing profits, as there is significant overlap between what is said and what is monetized) or are simply not regarded at all by those in positions of power. "Both sides" are simply treated differently. The result isn't just to obscure what should be a clear line between justice and dehumanization. It also lays the foundations for the existence of cancel culture: if the platforms won't intervene, the people will.

Opponents of cancel culture, of course, are quick to highlight the people whose lives have been upended by the wrath of the online mob. Sometimes this happens; sometimes people lose jobs or friends or social standing because of what they say online. Sometimes the punishment doesn't seem to match the crime, say when the offending comment is made out of ignorance or thoughtlessness rather than willful maliciousness. But as ten years of my research on online abuse, harassment, and media manipulation attest, the widespread, structural problem on social media is not people facing backlash for disagreeing with "progressive dogma," as comedian Ricky Gervais sneered in an interview with the *National Review*. Instead it is that platforms are calibrated to streamline the spread of sensationalism, falsehood, and harassment—harms that disproportionately affect marginalized communities online, just as environmental toxins in the sky, water, and soil disproportionately affect marginalized communities offline.

In an overwhelming number of cases, those who choose to harm and dehumanize, who make violent threats against vulnerable groups, and who trade in dangerous conspiracy theories, face zero consequences—most basically because they're often anonymous or pseudonymous, but also because the platforms refuse to step in and consistently enforce their own moderation policies. Many of these abusers are permitted—even outright incentivized—to build entire brands around hate. It took years and significant public pressure, for example, for Alex Jones's conspiracy theories, bigotry, and targeted abuse to finally warrant an intervention from the platforms. Moreover, these interventions often come with exploitable gray areas, or are otherwise rife with workarounds. For all of Facebook's talk about combatting white nationalism and supremacy, a recent investigation at the *Guardian* uncovered that white nationalists and supremacists are still operating openly on the platform. Sociologist Jessie Daniels explores a similar pattern on Twitter. As she argues, hate groups' longstanding reliance on the platform to organize and coordinate wide-scale attacks isn't some accident of history. "White supremacists love Twitter," Daniels states, "because it loves them back."

All the while, feminists, social justice activists, and community organizers are banned or have content removed, often without clear explanation, or for reasons not equally applied to far-right content. For example, black activists are regularly suspended for violating Facebook's hate speech standards. Their infraction? Using the word "black," or calling out racism. Suspensions of this kind are so common that activists have a name for it: getting "Zucked." On Instagram, queer and plus-sized users have been suspended and subjected to "shadow bans," meaning posts are hidden from view, for violating policies prohibiting "sexually suggestive" content—even when those queer and plus-sized bodies are fully clothed and not engaging in sexualized behavior. Similarly, Twitter applies its moderation policies unevenly and inexplicably, allowing deluge after deluge of misogynist attacks to remain up, but taking swift action against those most frequently targeted by all that abuse. For example, when a queer feminist filmmaker tweeted about a project titled "Love your cunt," which focused on body acceptance, their account was suspended within minutes for posting "hateful content."

This is where the arguments of cancel culture hand-wringers fall apart. "I'd say civilization moves forward when we embrace rule of law, not when we abandon it," David Brooks frets of the dangers of call-out culture. What Brooks fails to acknowledge is that, online, "rule of law" is not granted to certain populations.

These are precisely the kinds of institutional failures that Martin Luther King, Jr., highlighted in his 1963 "Letter from a Birmingham Jail." King's letter was directed to Birmingham's moderate white clergy members who, while professing support for the overall goals of the civil rights movement, urged activists to slow down, take a breath, and stop being so disruptive. Their actions were tearing Birmingham apart. Responding to the clergy's concerns about disturbing the city's peace, King conceded: "I would not hesitate to say that it is unfortunate that so-called demonstrations are taking place in Birmingham at this time. But I would say in more emphatic terms that it is even more unfortunate that the white power structure of this city left the Negro community with no other alternative."

No other alternative: for many segments of the population, this is a daily lived reality. No other alternative for responding to constant sexual abuse and harassment is why the Me Too movement, founded by black feminist Tarana Burke, took off the way it did. No other alternative for pushing back against white nationalist, xenophobic policies is why immigration and human rights activists use social media to organize and to make clear: no Muslim ban, no babies in cages, this country belongs to us, too. No other alternative for protecting black communities against police brutality and other forms of systemic violence is why Black Lives Matters exists as a movement. No other alternative for ensuring a safe and equitable learning environment is why students of color at my own institution,

Syracuse University, created the #NotAgainSU hashtag and staged a weeklong campus sit-in.

It should go without saying: not every action undertaken in the name of social justice is so pointed, or even particularly well thought-out; at a recent event, Barack Obama warned that being judgmental to strangers on the Internet should not be confused with serious activism. (Journalists quickly pounced on Obama's statements as a cancellation of cancel culture, although he only mentioned calling someone out in passing; his remarks were more focused on the political ineffectiveness of saying harsh words without following them up with meaningful action. Superficial wokeness, in other words. Still, that fit the tidy narrative that even Obama hates the screaming hoards.) Obviously, yelling one woke thing one time certainly doesn't an activist make. But that's not all that happens online, not by a long shot. A great deal of the behavior lumped under callout or cancel culture reflects deeply engaged, deeply thoughtful, deeply necessary civil rights activism both online and off—activism spurred by the fact that institutions have proven too slow or too disinterested or too worried about the bottom line to adequately address imminent threats against marginalized bodies.

Writing in the *New York Times*, Ta-Nehisi Coates offers a blunt assessment of how we got here. The new cancel culture—which differs from the old cancel culture, Coates explains, when the tool of cancellation was used exclusively by dominant voices to silence the marginalized—reflects a world in which the "great abuses" of racism and sexual violence and other systemic marginalizations are now put on display for all to see. The impulse to cancel and call out, he argues, are birthed from compounding institutional failures, hypocrisies, and "capricious and biased" uses of power. Earnest Owens elaborates, also in the *New York Times*: "As a millennial who has participated in using digital platforms to critique powerful people for promoting bigotry or harming others, I can assure you it wasn't because they had 'different opinions.' It was because they were spreading the kinds of ideas that contribute to the marginalization of people like me and those I care about. It was because I didn't want them to have a no-questions-asked platform to do this."

The claim that failed institutions spur vigorous, even vigilante, pushback isn't specific to cancel culture or the left, as Megan Ward and Jessica Beyer illustrate in a study of the effects of global disinformation. When people feel that no one else will intervene, they're inclined to take matters into their own hands.

Regarding identity-based harassment, violent bigotry, and disinformation online, it is not just that people *feel* abandoned by institutions. They *have* been abandoned, reflecting years of corporate decision-making that, as legal scholars Frank Pasquale and Danielle Keats Citron argue, maximizes harmful speech at the expense of public health. People can't count on Facebook or Twitter or Instagram or YouTube—to say nothing of the United States government, which is currently courting the likes of Mark Zuckerberg in a play to shore up political influence—to do the right thing. And so, they take up the cause themselves. Not every resulting call-out, invective, and campaign warrants unquestioning praise. What they all do warrant, however, is context, and a good-faith inquiry as to why it is happening.

FOR CRITICS OF CANCEL CULTURE, discussions of the pervasiveness—and in their view, the excesses—of cancellation often dovetail into lamentations about the death of civility. We used to be able to talk to each other, this argument goes, but now we can't. This is what makes the impulse to call out and cancel others so damaging. Instead of working through differences, people become heat-seeking missiles for anyone who disagrees.

Well, some people. In the ten years I've been doing this work, I've never seen anyone take a bigot to task because they're not using their inside voice. Instead, media coverage of white nationalists and supremacists during and after the 2016 election often marveled at how "polite" and "articulate" the racists were. This isn't a new framing; as Juan González and Joseph Torres explain in a history of race in U.S. media, journalists have long employed sympathetic language to describe white racial terrorists—including lynch mobs during Reconstruction and settlers who massacred Native Americans during U.S. colonialization—while simultaneously blaming their targets for the resulting violence.

Much contemporary news coverage replicates a similar dynamic, as those who have been directly targeted by violent bigots—or clap back when others are targeted, or refuse to sweep wrongdoing under the rug because some time has passed or the perpetrator swears they didn't *mean* any harm—are the ones most policed for their volume and tone. And not just policed; often decried as the problem itself.

The tendency to transform victims into victimizers feeds into calls for civility, which according to the *Atlantic*'s Van Newkirk have for generations been used by members of the dominant group to muffle the frustrations of the oppressed. Indeed, civility was explicitly weaponized to stymie the civil rights movement, which was denounced at the time as deeply uncivil by nervous whites who recoiled from the deliberately confrontational nature of the movement.

Also writing in the *Atlantic*, Adam Serwer zooms that historical camera out even further. As far back as Reconstruction, calls for civility have been tethered to disenfranchisement. After all, it's easy to discuss the "race problem" using calm inside voices when the only voices present are white, male, and personally unaffected by the threats to civil rights under discussion. In our present era, Serwer explains, lamentations about the loss of civility have a similarly antidemocratic undercurrent, pointing to a halcyon yesteryear when there were fewer voices at the table, and fewer restrictions on what those in power had to answer for. Civility then and civility now is an assertion of power, and an effort to maintain the status quo. It is best defined, Serwer says, not as "not being an asshole," but rather as "I can do what I want and you can shut up."

For all the pathos, disappointment, and often outright disgust projected onto those who opt for direct pushback against reactionary violence, little attention is paid to the subjective experiences of those doing the pushback—their feelings, their fears, their personal motivations. In contrast, those who target and terrorize marginalized bodies are approached as individuals who have stories to tell and grievances to take seriously. *Their* context, *their* reasons for acting the way they do, matter.

Black feminist scholar Brittney Cooper lays out the root of this discrepancy. There are different standards, she explains, for white anger and white fear, both of which are regarded as "honest" emotions. White anger is legitimized, contextualized, and traced back to past traumas, granting the white folks who feel it a de facto interiority. In contrast, nonwhite anger and fear is minimized, decried as irrational, or framed as an existential threat to the status quo. The only psychologizing it tends to generate is how white people feel about it.

The most obvious example is the deluge of coverage devoted to Trump's base during and after the 2016 election. Some coverage is, of course, appropriate. Trump won the presidency; Trump, his policies, and his supporters make news. But *some* coverage isn't what Trump supporters get. Instead, the interests of the pro-Trump minority—and it has only ever been a minority—are given an outsized amount of attention, coverage, and concern. MAGA anger comes from somewhere, and it is our job to get to the bottom of it. Very often, this means handing Trump supporters a microphone so they can explain—and justify—that anger themselves.

The myopic focus on white anger and fear is most conspicuous, and most insidious, the more dehumanizing and terrorizing the behaviors. Following mass shootings, for example, a familiar pattern emerges. The news media first focuses on the shooter's manifesto, his (and it is almost always a *his*) online activities, and the ubiquitous question: *Why did he do this?* Like clockwork, this reporting spurs a backlash from people such as myself who argue that we should not be oxygenating these views, we should not be handing these people a microphone to say anything. Then, there is the backlash to this backlash: we have to understand why this is happening. Light disinfects, this argument goes. If we don't crack the code of what inspires a person to pick up an assault weapon and aim it at mostly Mexican American families at a Walmart, we'll never figure out how to prevent future attacks.

It should go without saying that it is critical to understand the process of radicalization. It is critical to listen to scholars such as Daniels, whose work on the centrality of white supremacy within U.S. culture and the ways that digital spaces have long been havens for violent bigotry provides decades of context for the current far-right resurgence. But there is a big difference between analyzing the conditions that give rise to violent extremism and providing violent bigots a platform to plead their case and their humanity—especially when it comes at the expense of providing a platform to the voices and the humanity of the people they terrorize.

THIS HIERARCHY OF PERSONHOOD plays out in much more subtle ways online. When people who have long been abandoned by institutions take matters into their own hands and name and shame bigots, or unmask serial sexual abusers, or mete out some other punishment for behaviors that threaten public health, the knee-jerk response is to lump their calls together and condemn it as toxic, cruel, and dangerous to democracy. Their anger is perceived as out of control, irredeemable, not worth considering other than to condemn it. Why bother? These are people whose interiority is irrelevant.

Simultaneously, the rise of the so-called "alt-right" online has spurred a cottage industry of analysis, interest, and armchair psychologizing in an effort to "understand" their anger. "In the future," Daniels tweeted in October 2019, following the release of yet another page-turner about white supremacists, "everyone will be famous for 15 minutes for a book on the alt-right." Their interiority *is* relevant. Let's listen carefully.

In his op-ed, Brooks lamented that "even the quest for justice can turn into barbarism if it is not infused with a quality of mercy, an awareness of human frailty and a path to redemption." Brooks is right; what's missing from discourses around call-out and cancel culture is holistic, fully contextualized understanding. What he's wrong about is the direction the barbarism is traveling when only certain people are given that grace—when the motivations, anxieties, and built-up anger of the victimizers are treated *more* mercifully than those of the victimized.

The irony, of course, is that failing—or outright refusing—to see both sides of the "both sides" debate deepens the anger of those condemned to invisibility. It also reinforces targeted people's need for aggressive grassroots pushback against bigots and their apologists—both witting and unwitting. If you truly want to do something about cancel culture, take the radical step of doing what you do for everyone else. See them.

RIGHTEOUS INCIVILITY
Amy Olberding

PUBLIC DISCOURSE is in an accelerating downward spiral of coarse insult, free-flying contempt, and general meanness. We will surely soon reach bottom, an inevitably inarticulate resting place where we quit wasting words and just mutely flip each other off. Since bemoaning our uncivil culture is almost as prevalent as incivility itself, let me forgo any ritual hand-wringing. I register the culture here because it so influences me: as public discourse grows crueler, nastier, and more aggressive, my temptations to be uncivil increase apace, and I don't like that.

My growing temptations to incivility are diverse and predictable. When one encounters disrespect, the desire to answer in kind is strong. Likewise, with so many pitched to provoke anger, one wants to give them just the outrage they invite. More basically, I find it ever harder to like people and so to act as if I like them—misanthropy does not seem so unreasonable as it once did. But incivility's most powerful appeal is that it can seem downright righteous.

The desire to be civil, in its cleanest and most robust form, is a desire to be *moral*, to treat others humanely, with respect, toleration, and consideration. But if one wants to be moral, one must also know that, in order to be good, sometimes one cannot be nice. The imperative to treat others civilly is never responsibly total because sometimes a moral good is won in rudeness. To display disrespect or enmity, to mock or shun, to insult or shame—these can be moral gestures. For even as we need to respect humanity, valuing human beings can sometimes require disrespecting some of them, precisely the ones who deny or damage our shared humanity. To show such people respect and consideration might let them have their way a bit, let them continue in their destructive ways.

My sneering contempt for your terrible moral outlook might not stop you, but maybe my disdain can slow you down or discourage others from doing like you do. This, then, is where temptation is at its greatest. There are many who do not so much succumb, but actively embrace it. The world at present is not just full of rude people, it is full of people being rude because they judge it to be righteous. I feel the pull. But I have doubts.

I BELIEVE THAT RIGHTEOUS INCIVILITY is sometimes better than civility and that it can indicate a pattern of reasoning we morally need. Civility typically requires conformity to social conventions that symbolically signal prosocial values; we follow customs of courtesy to display respect, consideration, and toleration for each other. But, as philosopher Cheshire Calhoun observes, morally mature people don't just run on conformity—they also reason. They will have a "socially critical moral point of view," she writes, an ability to develop values independent of social customs and conventions. When we experience a tension between conformity to convention and individual moral conviction, we will sometimes resolve it in favor of conviction—we decline to conform because we judge it morally better not to.

Having a strongly held, independent moral conviction does not inevitably prompt incivility—I can civilly disagree with what I judge wrong—but sometimes moral convictions can make more seem necessary. I need not just to object or dissent, but to disrespect and show it. Civility would have me shake your hand, but my conscience can revolt and rebel. If I in fact refuse to shake your hand, I won't just be rude: I will take myself to be *righteously* rude. I disrupt the usual civil patterns because I morally judge they *need* disrupting, whether because integrity demands it or because some greater social good is won by it, or both. This pattern of reasoning is one we certainly need, lest we become unthinking conformists to superficial forms of niceness that would sacrifice higher values.

My doubts about righteous incivility are not about whether it is sometimes best but about how to tell when that would be so. The abstract case I make for it leaves out the gnarly mess of how my motivations work. I can tell myself I want what is good and right, but there is often more that I want as well. Civility entails restraint and this alone can make one want to fail it, for failure here is sweet release, a liberation one can like, and like too much. Awful people are just awful and there is a giddy, triumphal pleasure in announcing just how low they sit in my opinion. If I really don't respect you, it feels quite good to deny you the conventions that conceal disdain. In short, the pleasure of incivility is a heady part of its appeal. Other parts of its appeal are discovered best in hindsight.

What I tell myself is righteous incivility is sometimes little more than ugly mood or bad attitude. I alibi my uncivil crimes by claiming to sit in a moral space of reasons while I am really elsewhere— perhaps reveling in foul temperament, swimming in annoyance, or joyfully putting a boot on your neck simply because I dislike you. Later reflection will expose the ruse and I will see that the mood I called "righteous" is better called "angry," "irritable," "impatient" or just "tired." There was no commanding moral good I sought through incivility. That was just the story I told myself so I could set my inner junkyard dog off the leash.

My mixed motivations make me distrust my "righteously uncivil" impulses. One need not be puritanical or precious about what can motivate moral action to be suspicious when the "righteous" brings pleasure and relief or lets me lash and thrash where I like. Episodic self-deception will likely always be a risk when I am rude—I sometimes know better what I do only once I've done it—but I lately find myself prey to self-deception of a more systematic sort. I am encouraged to righteous incivility by forces greater than my own messy internal workings, by both other people and our public culture.

I used to think that, were I self-deceived, other people would be my help—after all, when one is wrong about oneself or what one does, other people tend to work as a quick but painful check. This is why Jean-Paul Sartre claims that hell is other people: they'll reject the fictions that you tell yourself or even announce plainly where you err. This lately happens less to me than I can trust. The hellish sorts are now too easy to evade. Let me illustrate my trouble.

There are loads of people whose values and conduct I disdain. I could right now take this fact to Facebook and deliver it, fantastically, to others: *These miserable assholes need to fuck right off and die!* I know exactly what would follow: lots of "likes," as well as comments that align with mine and escalate the ire. There would be humor in abundance—indicting ribaldry about *them*, fantasized rough fates that *they* deserve. If *they* chime in to protest, they'll quickly be subdued with more and worse, or I can always cut them off, unfriend them for their failure to accept the contempt I think their due. Any milder sorts reluctant to accept my claims or methods will of course pass on in silence. If they doubt my views or vehemence, they'll keep that to themselves, lest they too become my target. So, when the dust has settled, I will come away assured that I am righteous, that I have stood for good and justly trampled bad. The experience will flatter my self-perception and help me fit myself inside the stories that our wider culture tells, all the many ways we valorize that rudeness we think righteous.

Popular rhetoric often depicts the righteously uncivil person as the brave iconoclast, one who heroically refuses the dissembling and pretense that stand between ourselves and the true, the right, and the good. The uncivil person will be lauded for "keeping things real," exercising a gritty rejection of polite fakery in order to say exactly what he thinks. He might be praised as "politically incorrect," resolutely free from any forced and false consensus to which the cowardly rest submit. Or perhaps he valiantly "speaks truth to power," audaciously defiant of what power can do. The metaphors that suit him best are martial. Where others cushion criticism with softening tact, he "takes the gloves off" to deliver truth bare-knuckled. He "calls out" others' errors as a duelist would, issuing a public challenge that will force their choice between open confrontation or humiliated retreat. He plainly "punches," though always in a noble way, "punching up" but never "down," ever sure that he can sort the "up" from the "down." When I am righteously uncivil, I can cast myself in any of these ways. I become a fierce combatant righting all that's wrong. And I have unappealing stories I can tell about any who object.

Incivility requires strength and valor, but those who dislike it are frail and fragile. The offended like apologies but what they really need is to "man up," "toughen up" and grow a "thicker skin," one that can better stand a lashing. They're as delicate as "snowflakes," melting in the slightest heat. Protesting incivility is weakness—pathetic whining or mewling infantilism. Or maybe it's a bovine nature, a sign you live inside that unthinkingly conformist "herd." Perhaps most basically of all, if my rough uncivil truths about your bad character or actions injure your pride, you have yourself to blame. Err less and save yourself the pain of my correction; stop being awful, and I will stop pointing it out.

This style of talk infects my temptations to incivility. I can be unfettered from restraint and speak as rudely as I find. That plenty of people will both like and "like" it reassures me that I am right, that my blows land on targets that need a little roughing up. Temptation can grow total and I will think: *Fuck civility*—not just now but always.

When you know what's right and good and true, take off the gloves and punch for it. Make this your habit and your way—why not? We have enough of the potent awful, and of the impotent but "nice." Let me be the virtuous, righteously uncivil hero. This, I think, is the siren song of systematic self-deception, of righteous incivility's near enemy.

THOSE WHO AIM FOR VIRTUE try to steer away from vice. "Pursue the good, avoid the bad," we tell ourselves, but bad will sometimes look like good. The good can have what Buddhaghosa, the Indian Buddhist philosopher from the fifth century CE, calls "near enemies." Virtues, Buddhaghosa argues, do not simply have corresponding vices, they also have near enemies—seductive, plausible counterfeits that closely resemble the virtues but are nonetheless distortions of it. This is why, he explains, we can mistake indifference for equanimity, or attachment for love. These can look alike, and the risk is that we aim for one but hit the other. Worse still, because of their resemblance, we can call a bullseye when we miss. I can think I have achieved the unperturbed poise of equanimity when in fact I simply fail to care enough—I enjoy the dubious peace that indifference to the world and all its woes can bring. The near enemy is a far more subtle form of error than plain vice, for it is moral failure taken as success.

Buddhaghosa does not speak of righteous incivility or what its near enemy might be. But my doubts about my uncivil impulses concern how an eager, open, pugilistic temper is read not just as righteous but as heroic. Was valor ever so easy or so fun? Since I have a taste for "keeping things real," I best start being real with myself. Popular heroics are seductive, but they are not reliably righteous. Incivility can quiet critics and earn praise from friends, but neither mean I'm right or righteous. The social feedback that I get might not only fail to point to good, it could just be my problem. Where is hell when you really need it? I am trying to find it in myself.

A righteously uncivil person would, I think, care to make a difference. Where she finds wrong, she'll want it righted. But that is rarely how the "righteous" incivilities I see and practice work. The language that we use itself reveals the challenge. I can uncivilly punch but, for this to work a change, the one I punch must come to understand both that she deserved it and why—the punched must be persuaded. In my more reflective moments, I recognize the psychological implausibility of this posture. It takes a hardy moral character to receive a slap as a summons to be good. But why would I think that one so low in my opinion will not just rise but soar to heights of circumspection, receiving disrespect as a provocation to be better? If she's bad enough to need a punch, she's not likely good enough to take it well and change. The far more likely outcome is that she'll answer like with like, return the punch, and we together will descend at speed into a gutter war for social dominance. "Victory" will come when one of us is cowed enough at last to quit—no one changed, all bloodied.

If my pugilism won't change the punched, perhaps the difference I can make lies with those outside the ring. This at least is the reasoning that we sometimes give. When we "speak truth to power," for example, we lay claim to helping those without it—the punch is not aggression but defense. The righteously uncivil would here indeed seem to be heroic, but that's the rub where my motivations are concerned. Using incivility in defense of others is reasoning I can like, but maybe what I like is how it honors my pretensions. The risk is that I valorize myself as specially righteous where power is concerned, all the while neglecting what a form of power righteous posturing can be.

If you will "speak truth to power," it will help a lot if you also speak *from* power. Some of us, let's face it, cannot really pull this off. We might get fired from our jobs or alienate people that we really need. Some of us can try for righteous incivility but fail because of who we are and how our incivilities will read socially. Uncivil black men will not be taken as refreshingly "real," but instead as threatening or dangerous; the economically poor might well be taken as "punching," but that's because they are, as we'd expect, trashy, brutish, and coarse. All of this is but to say that the fine and noble qualities I can claim in righteous incivility—my independence and my courage—are qualities not really mine or earned. They are instead propped up by a social system that lets those most free be freest with their rudeness. Because of this, my roaring impulses to deliver righteous punches are haunted by the whispered thought: *Just look at what I get to do.* And then self-doubting questions come: When I count myself the righteously uncivil warrior, have I challenged or changed the hierarchies of power? Or have I just enacted them? That some will see me as I wish, as the hero I would be, is no help with this.

Alongside the heroic stories I might tell about my boldly uncivil defense of the powerless are other, less attractive stories. Philosophers Brandon Warmke and Justin Tosi offer one that makes me squirm. "Moral grandstanding," they write, is a distinctive form of communication that "aims to convince others that one is 'morally respectable.'" It transpires when we advertise our moral convictions to others, hoping thereby to gain greater regard or to secure in-group belonging. Moral grandstanding—related to "virtue signaling"—need not of course be uncivil, but I expect it often is. Uncivilly punching at the wrong and bad can well display that I am right and good. Indeed, that I show outrage so intense it overmasters all civility is potent proof of this, a way to pose as so distressed by vice that my virtue must show as rude.

Moral grandstanding and virtue signaling are most often used as weapons in the wider wars—they are handy accusations I can hurl at others when they morally opine in ways I don't like. A far better use of these concepts, though a use no one can like, is to turn them, weapon-like, upon oneself. What if the incivilities I call righteous are a form of self-promotion, a way to seek approval and esteem? What if they merely confess insecurity that I belong among the moral? If I really would be righteous, I need to ask this of myself, I think. Therapeutic cynicism about my motives might help me see when I don't really act on conviction but instead seek to parade it. Worse still, it makes me reconsider just what might form my aversion to the civil.

Civil persuasion is a nasty sort of business, one that offers few heroics. It takes patience, care, and work. It entails getting my hands dirty by trying to reason long and hard with others I often cannot like. It draws little admiration in an age like ours, little I can celebrate as triumph over all that is bad and wrong. It could even lose me the esteem of those who share my values—they might well find in my politeness a tolerance for wrong. At the very least, I'll lose the ribald joys I often get when me and mine take down you and yours, the atavistic satisfactions of the brawl. Civility is not at all seductive as a habit or a plan, yet I think the pull of the seductive is my problem. Near enemies exercise appeal. They take the superficial signs of goodness for the thing itself—bathetic, cheap heroics that others cheer stand in for whatever it might really mean to win some better world.

I doubt I can enumerate what genuinely righteous incivility would require, though I still believe it to exist. I doubt that it will match what I am often like when I think my rudeness righteous. I doubt it will be joyous or triumphal, that it will summon up attention and approval, or that it will show up dressed in self-valorizing, violent language. I doubt it will find satisfaction in the pain and shame provoked in others. Most of all, I suspect it will involve regret.

Truly righteous incivility would issue from a deeply moral wish against its own necessity. It would come about as forced, a sorry step one feels reluctantly obliged to take. Morally good people *want* to respect others—they want a world in which we can, in all good conscience and effect, treat each other humanely and kindly. They do not want to signal disrespect even when they see they must. They are people who perceive a moral need to be rough and inconsiderate as distressing or at least a disappointment. Perhaps my disappointment in myself, in my too-eager impulse for the punch, can be used to turn me toward this better form of disappointment.

This essay was originally published in Aeon (aeon.co).

CONTRIBUTORS

Rachel Achs is a PhD candidate in philosophy at Harvard University.

Paul Bloom is the Brooks and Suzanne Ragen Professor of Psychology at Yale and author of *Against Empathy: The Case for Rational Compassion.*

Elizabeth Bruenig is a columnist at the *Washington Post.*

Judith Butler is the Maxine Elliot Professor in the Department of Comparative Literature and the Program of Critical Theory at UC Berkeley and author of *The Force of Nonviolence: The Ethical in the Political.*

Agnes Callard is Associate Professor of Philosophy at the University of Chicago.

Daryl Cameron is Assistant Professor in the Department of Psychology and ethics core faculty member in the Rock Ethics Institute.

Myisha Cherry is Assistant Professor of Philosophy at UC Riverside and author of *UnMuted: Conversations on Prejudice, Oppression, and Social Justice.*

Barbara Herman is the Griffin Professor of Philosophy and Professor of Law at UCLA and author of *Moral Literacy.*

Desmond Jagmohan is Assistant Professor of Political Science at UC Berkeley.

David Konstan is Professor of Classics at New York University and author of *In the Orbit of Love: Affection in Ancient Greece and Rome.*

Oded Na'aman is a fellow of the Martin Buber Society at the Hebrew University of Jerusalem.

Martha C. Nussbaum, Ernst Freund Distinguished Service Professor of Law and Ethics at the University of Chicago, is author of *The Cosmopolitan Tradition: A Noble but Flawed Ideal.*

Amy Olberding is the Presidential Professor of Philosophy at the University of Oklahoma. Her latest book is *The Wrong of Rudeness.*

Whitney Phillips, Assistant Professor of Communication, Culture, and Digital Technologies at Syracuse University, is author of *This Is Why We Can't Have Nice Things.*

Jesse Prinz is Distinguished Professor of Philosophy at the Graduate Center, CUNY, and author of *The Conscious Brain.*

Victoria Spring is a PhD candidate in social psychology at Pennsylvania State University.

Brandon M. Terry, Assistant Professor of African and African American Studies and Social Studies at Harvard University, is coeditor of *To Shape a New World: The Political Philosophy of Martin Luther King, Jr.*